THE UNIVERSITY OF
WINCHESTER

Martial Rose Library
Tel: 01962 827306

- 5 DEC 2008

- 1 OCT 2012

YOUNG BILINGUAL LEARNERS
AT HOME AND SCHOOL
researching multilingualism

26 FEB 2009

- 1 OCT 2012

2 6 NOV 2010

2 4 FEB 2011

2 7 FEB 2012

SEVEN DAY LOAN ITEM

To be returned on or before the day marked above, subject to recall.

D1427201

YOUNG BILINGUAL LEARNERS
AT HOME AND SCHOOL
researching multilingual voices

Rose Drury

Trentham Books

Stoke on Trent, UK and Sterling, USA

Trentham Books Limited
Westview House   22883 Quicksilver Drive
734 London Road   Sterling
Oakhill   VA 20166-2012
Stoke on Trent   USA
Staffordshire
England ST4 5NP

© 2007 Rose Drury

First published 2007

British Library Cataloguing-in-Publication Data
A catalogue record for this book is available from the British Library

ISBN-13: 978 1 85856 355 8

Designed and typeset by Trentham Print Design Ltd, Chester and
printed in Great Britain by Cromwell Press Ltd, Trowbridge.

Contents

Dedication

To Isabel and Alexander

Acknowledgements

This book is the result of researching young bilingual children's learning at home and at school over many years. I am grateful to a number of people who encouraged me to write this book.

First and foremost I am indebted to the children, Samia, Maria and Nazma, their families and teachers who invited me into their homes and classrooms and participated in the research. Their stories are the subject of the book.

I learnt a great deal from the University of London language and culture research group and my work gained strength from sharing understandings with fellow researchers in our field. I particularly appreciated the support of friends and colleagues in NALDIC (National Association for Language Development in the Curriculum) over the years.

I would like to thank my colleagues in the Watford Section 11 team and Pre-school project for their invaluable insights into the children's learning which helped to shape my research. Hugh's understanding and involvement is particularly significant. I am also grateful for the support from the Minority Ethnic Curriculum Support Service, Hertfordshire and from the Department of Education, University of Hertfordshire during the course of my research study.

I am particularly indebted to my friend and colleague, Mussarat. Without her trust and understanding my study of three bilingual girls in Watford would not have been possible.

Finally, I would like to acknowledge the inspirational guidance and friendship of Eve, who has always believed in the importance of my work and has taught me so much.

During the final stages of this book, I owe a great deal to David's patience and encouragement. The final proof reading and index for the book have been expertly undertaken by my friend Cressida. And to Gillian I am especially grateful. Her sensitive editing and belief in the message of the book have been invaluable.

My sincere thanks to you all.

Introduction

This book tells the story of three young bilingual children's learning at home and at nursery. It explores ethnographic approaches to listening, understanding and responding to young bilingual children's voices. It is also the story of being a researcher. The challenges presented by children whose voices and everyday lives are often viewed as invisible by early years practitioners can be understood through the multilingual methodologies explored in this book. Following socio-cultural approaches, these methodologies provide windows onto young bilingual children's learning and shed light on ways in which they participate in and contribute to multiple communities. These ethnographic methodologies capture the multilingual voices of three 4 year-old bilingual children at home and at school during their nursery education and help to provide a fuller and richer picture of bilingual children's learning.

We enter the story with an interview conducted at home with one of the children, Nazma, and her older sister, Naseem.

Interview – Nazma 6 years on

I returned to Nazma's home six years after concluding my research to discuss her memories of early schooling. Nazma sat with her elder sister, Naseem (aged 16), during the interview. Nazma is now just 10 years old and in Year 5 of her primary school.

[R = Rose, N = Nazma, Nas = Naseem]

R   What do you remember about nursery?

N: It's this big place and lots of corners

R: What was it like when you first went into nursery? What did it feel like?

N: Scary

R: Why was it scary?

N: Because this teacher, Mrs Offley, shouted at me 'cos sometimes she used to shout at me because I never used to speak to her

R: Why didn't you speak to her?

N: I was shy with the teachers

R: Did you speak to anyone?

N: I speak to Mussarat.

Naseem's comments:

[she has been sitting listening to Nazma's conversation]

Nas: She's always been a quiet person

She talks to herself for hours

When I went to the parent consultation meeting, they were happy

They said she is doing fine

They said she is still very quiet

She's still the baby

I think that might be the reason why she was so quiet because she was the baby

I think she was really attached to my mum

I think that's what made her scared

And also in the Asian community you don't really mix with other people

I think she feel frightened

Some children in nursery have really strong characters and she was really quiet

That's why she got scared

Being in the house just tucked away, then with everyone and I think the best solution for her was to shut herself up.

R: Can you see yourself in her experience?

Nas: I was very much like that as well

I was very closed

I was very shy speaking to teachers, but thinking back now, I think that's really stupid

They've only teachers, but you felt that everything you're going to say, it's going to come out wrong and everyone looking at you

It's getting that confidence

And I suppose you get that when you are growing up and mixing with new people and socialising

It must have been very difficult for Mrs Offley. She was used to children who talked a lot and had strong characters

But Nazma just kept herself to herself

This is very striking. Firstly we see Nazma's ability to reflect on and express her feelings about nursery experience in a way that could not have been articulated at the time of her early schooling. This provides an additional insight into Nazma's learning world. Naseem states clearly at the end of the interview, 'Nazma just kept herself to herself' and we begin to understand the power of the 'silent period' in Nazma's early learning of English. She felt under pressure to speak to teachers, was socially isolated and 'was shy with the teachers.' But she had come to understand the significance of responding appropriately to teachers. Overall, nursery to Nazma was a 'scary place' where teachers 'shouted' at her and she responded by taking the easiest solution, as her sister observed, 'to shut herself up.' Naseem also recognises the challenge faced by the nursery teacher, 'It must have been very difficult for Mrs Offley. She was used to children who talked a lot.'

Secondly, we have in Nazma a mirror image of her older sister at 10 years old and vice versa. Naseem states, 'I was very much like that as well'. Thus we recognise a pattern set from the earliest days in school. During my visit Naseem noted that she had left school with no GCSEs or other qualifications. At 16 she was now helping her mother at home and, if this image of Naseem were to become a reality for Nazma as well, she would not have met her mother's high expectations of her. So this longitudinal ethnographic study of young children at home and at school is not only about Nazma finding her way through nursery, but also about life chances and meeting inequalities that Nazma and Naseem face during their early schooling. And more, it is about giving a voice to children and their families, like those of Nazma and Naseem, which otherwise might not be heard.

The book is organised in two parts.

In Part One, the context for researching and understanding young bilingual children's learning at home and at school is introduced through the stories of Nazma, Samia and Maria.

The book opened with an interview with Nazma which illustrates some of the challenges facing bilingual children and their teachers in the early years of schooling. In Chapter 1 the context for the three girls' learning is presented through their home experiences and their mothers' perspectives.

Chapter 2 explores ethnographic approaches to listening, understanding and responding to young bilingual children's voices. Through the story of the processes involved in researching Nazma, Samia and Maria, we seek answers to the central question of the book: what is the experience of young bilingual children as they start formal schooling?

In Chapter 3 the children's experiences of early schooling are presented through nursery vignettes, Baseline Assessment scores and the nursery teachers' views of their learning. This 'visible' learning is set in the context of current policy and practice in respect of young children for whom English is an additional language.

These first chapters set the context for Nazma, Samia and Maria as they enter the new cultural and linguistic world of early schooling. How Nazma, Samia and Maria make their way as they come to terms with the reality of learning a new language in a new social, cultural and linguistic setting, is discussed in Part Two, beginning with Chapter 4.

The key theoretical frameworks which help us understand young bilingual children's learning at home and at school are outlined. The socio-cultural perspectives emphasise the role of the child in her own learning and include a new interpretation of the child as mediator, playing an active role during the silent period of the early stages of her learning of English.

The theme is developed in Chapters 5 and 6 as the children make their way through early schooling and respond strategically to their experiences – at nursery in Chapter 5 and at home in Chapter 6. This is the Inner Layer, or invisible learning which demonstrates how Nazma, Samia and Maria find their own way through the different contexts.

Finally, in Chapter 7, the implications for the education of young bilingual children are considered. What can we learn from the stories of Nazma, Samia and Maria's invisible learning?

This book includes examples from the children's bilingual voices. In the text all talk in Pahari, the children's mother tongue, translated into English is presented in italics, and English in Roman script.

PART ONE

SETTING THE CONTEXT: RESEARCHING YOUNG BILINGUAL CHILDREN'S LEARNING

1
The story of my children

A mother's view of her daughter's early schooling:
'*I don't know about school, but the teachers know how to help my daughter.*'
[Interview with Nazma's mother]

The origins of my research

The story of three young bilingual girls' learning is told through the story of my research. It originated with a small-scale study of bilingual pupils' underachievement at a multi-ethnic primary school in Watford near London. This study provided a new insight into the learning experiences of bilingual children at home and at school and, significantly, introduced me to Naseem, her family and her little sister, Nazma. It was during the process of developing my study that the real inquiry began. The need to understand the experiences of Nazma as she started her schooling became fascinating. The child I had met at home with her mother, siblings and extended family, was about to make the most important transition, in terms of her educational attainment and future life chances, as she entered nursery.

In my earlier professional role, as leader of an innovative Pre-school Community-based project, I worked with bilingual outreach assistants in the homes of young children from minority language communities. Its aim, to improve opportunities for bilingual children to succeed in the school system, had led me back to Nazma and her family. I developed a deeper understanding of the families and their pre-school children within their home context. This presented a view of the child which was in sharp contrast to that of their nursery teachers, the Baseline Assessment scores and, most significantly, the nursery experiences of the children themselves. At home Nazma was viewed as an active learner, talking and playing in a culturally and linguistically appropriate way. For Nazma and her educators, the constraints set by the expectations, rules and language of instruction set an enormous challenge. I met Samia and Maria later, during my visits to the homes of other families involved in the Pre-school Project. All three girls shared the same linguistic and cultural heritage. Their families originated from Azad Kashmir and were now part of the settled community in Watford. They all began their school careers at the same time, each with high hopes and expectations. My research closely documented their first year in nursery and tracked their experiences and achievements as they progressed through the schooling system.

I came to realise that despite their limited understanding of the language and culture of their new school environment, all three girls were able to take control of their learning, both at home and at school. This became a central insight of my study and contrasts with a prevalent view that young bilingual learners who are at an early stage in their learning of English are at the mercy of linguistic, cultural and social forces over which they have no control. The reality of their experience, as I came to understand it, was much more complex. One significant piece of data was 'Samia and Sadaqat playing school' (see end of chapter 2). In the early days of the study, collection of home data was difficult. It was intended to secure the most naturalistic data possible in order to develop in-depth perspectives on the children's home and school learning. The recording of Samia playing her 'school game' with her little brother provide unique insights into this process. Moreover it confirmed the success of the data collection process and became the trigger for much of the data analysis. Exposing this invisible learning is intended to give a voice to significant aspects of the children's learning experiences which otherwise might not have been heard.

I have shared the story of Nazma with early years practitioners, through publications and talks. Highlighting aspects of her experience during her early days at school has provided an opportunity for valuable reflection in support of promoting changes in practice to meet the needs of young bilingual children more satisfactorily. I am reminded of an article I read in the 1980s entitled 'Rehana's Reception' (1984), which had a profound impact on my thinking. It sets out the experience of Rehana, a 5 year-old bilingual child, as she starts school:

> For small children school can be a terrifying and confusing experience. For children who have little understanding of English, it is even more terrifying and confusing. It could be argued that Rehana was lucky – her sister was already in the school, her teacher was patient and sympathetic, the other chil-

dren were not particularly hostile. Many 5 year olds don't experience such a favourable start. But why is school so terrifying for so many children?

There is very little training for them [school support staff] and they are left to intuit the ethos of the school. This process is too haphazard for Rehana and all other children like her.' (Anon: 1984)

Over twenty years later, my study raises similar issues, particularly in relation to current training for early years educators.

Nazma's older sister: raising questions

In the late twentieth century, there was increasing awareness of under-achievement for a substantial number of bilingual children in Watford schools. It seemed particularly the case for children from Azad Kashmiri backgrounds and followed a recognisable pattern. These bilingual children entering nursery or Reception classes, whose early socialisation had taken place only in their mother tongue, experienced an abrupt change in both language and cultural expectations. In a totally English language environment, they became effectively dispossessed of their ability to communicate. By the end of their first year of formal schooling, we observed the children slowly acquiring some English but at the same time beginning to lose their mother tongue. As they moved through Key Stage One, these children appeared to develop a degree of fluency in English for social purposes, on a more superficial level ('playground English'), but it became apparent at Key Stage Two that they had difficulties responding to the increasing literacy and cognitive demands of the curriculum, so had little chance of success in secondary school. Was it this mismatch between home and school expectations, as well as a discontinuity of learning because of their inability to use mother tongue or English for academic purposes, that led to difficulties and underachievement in their early years of schooling?

I was interested in the factors which influence levels of achievement of bilingual children from the Azad Kashmiri community and began a survey of bilingual pupils in one multi-ethnic primary school in Watford. It focused on the learning of the bilingual pupils and explored factors affecting their achievement and underachievement from four different viewpoints: the pupil; the classteacher; classroom observer and parent.

The pilot study became the trigger for the in-depth study of young bilingual children's learning at home and at nursery, and Naseem was a specific case study.

Naseem: a case study

As an underachiever, Naseem was of particular interest. When I first met her, she was in Year 4. She appeared to be very conscious of her difficulties at school and was clearly underachieving. But when I visited her at home and talked to her mother, quite different views of her as a learner began to emerge. The following observation is drawn from interviews with Naseem and her mother.

> Her mother thinks that Naseem is doing very well at school. She shares responsibilities with her older sister, Zakkia, helping their mother with the younger children and the housework. She reads letters and explains the school newsletter to her, writes shopping lists, takes her shopping, and helps at the doctor's. Naseem brings books home from school to read. Her mother thinks she reads and writes well and she asks a wide range of questions. After school, she attends Qur'anic classes and also reads Arabic verses with her mother at home. Her mother has had no contact with the school apart from written school reports which say 'she is fine'. Mother is very keen to support her children with their school work, but she explains 'I am sorry I cannot help them because I am unable to communicate with the teachers in English. If I am worried, I just think about it, but I feel I can't do anything about it. I trust the school and if there is a problem, the school will let us know. So I don't want to make a fuss.'

What is striking is her view that Naseem is 'doing well', when her school experience is otherwise. Observations made in her classroom over time are noted below. Naseem is nine years old and in a Year 4 class in the school.

> The session starts with a whole class discussion about geography work on the British Isles. Naseem sits with a group of friends, passive and disengaged. The class returns to their desks to continue with on-going classwork, begun earlier in the week. The task is to complete a worksheet on the countries of the British Isles, to calculate the area of each using squared paper and to answer questions about the map. Most of the children in the class are working in pairs or small groups, but Naseem is sitting on her own. She has been working on this worksheet for several days, but is still counting the small squares on the map surface of each country and finding the task difficult. During the session, she becomes easily distracted and is off-task for much of the time. She sits for long spells of time neither engaged in the work nor asking for help from the classteacher or her peers. Later in the afternoon session she is tackling the worksheet, and it is evident that the question 'How many times bigger than Northern Ireland is the Republic of Ireland?' is difficult for her to understand. She sits at her desk with her hand held up, asking for help. After several minutes the classteacher asks the class to tidy up. The children assemble on the carpet at the end of the afternoon and go home. (Drury, 1997)

Naseem had attended school from nursery to Year 4. It was evident from her response to this Geography lesson that she was struggling with the demands of the curriculum. The task required an understanding of both the content – a knowledge of the countries in the British Isles, and the linguistic demand – how many times bigger than Northern Ireland is the Republic of Ireland? and also made mathematical demands – calculating the area of the map surface. The way that conceptualising problems may be closely related to English language development is illustrated through her difficulty in understanding the question about the relative size of Northern Ireland and the Republic of Ireland. Naseem was aware of her difficulties: she did not understand the classwork and said, 'I get shy sometimes (in the whole class context) and I don't know what to say because I might be wrong.' She had developed counter strategies to disengage from classroom tasks, avoiding interaction with the classteacher or her peers. At this stage, she knew that she was having little success. Yet by putting up her hand she acknowledged that she needed help, but she hadn't the confidence to be proactive in helping herself. Her attempt to engage in the task, her limited understanding, partial disengagement, her inability to secure help and the resulting failure to complete the task had become a familiar cycle to Naseem. Her self-esteem as a learner was low.

Naseem's classteacher, who recognised her underachievement in all areas of the curriculum, said that she had no self-belief, lacked confidence and was convinced that she could not do the classwork. She did not ask for help and 'needed a great deal of support in class.'

Her classteacher saw that Naseem could achieve some success if she had sufficient repetition and visual clues plus additional support from second language support staff, though he felt she would probably meet failure in secondary school. He had had no contact at all with her parents and no evidence of their support for her learning at school.

The questions raised by the findings point to factors that might have contributed to Naseem's difficulties at school and how her early learning experiences might have influenced her subsequent underachievement at school.

Naseem's younger sister, Nazma was about to embark upon her first experience of early schooling, and my questioning turned towards her. I believed at the time that while Naseem's situation may not necessarily have represented a mirror image of where Nazma would be in five years time, it was likely that the experience of the two sisters would be similar. The interview at the beginning of this book bears this out.

The nature of Naseem's underachievement was common to bilingual children from similar backgrounds in her school and in others. A particularly critical period for these children comes when they start formal schooling in the nursery, when they have to adjust immediately from home to school. Two aspects of this adjustment are crucial. First is the need to change from the mother tongue used in the home, to English used in school. Second is the shift from early socialisation at home to socialisation in school. To understand this process, we now follow the experiences of three young bilingual children as they start nursery.

Nazma, Samia and Maria
Invisible learning at home
The stories of Samia, Maria and Nazma, their families and their experiences at home are the subject of the book. As our study expands, we first uncover crucial aspects of the individual children's learning which might not be visible to their teachers or understood by policy makers. Secondly, we witness their early schooling according to their mothers' view of the children's overall development in both English and mother tongue.

Nazma at home
Nazma was the youngest of six children. She lived with her mother, father, grandmother and siblings. Her siblings attended the local primary and secondary school. Her eldest sister left school with no qualifications, and did not have a job. Nazma's father came to Watford in the 1960s and had received his schooling there. He too had no qualifications and became a driving instructor. He spoke Pahari and communicated well in English. Nazma's mother attended primary school in Azad Kashmir, married there and came to Watford in 1977. She spoke Pahari but little English.

Nazma and her siblings were born in Watford. Her early socialisation was centred at home with her parents, grandparents and other members of her extended family. She had not attended a playgroup or any pre-school setting in this country so her early learning experiences came from playing with siblings and other members of the extended family. Nazma's mother stated that Nazma enjoyed dressing-up and taking part in role play activities with siblings at home, particularly Yasmin. She enjoyed sorting clothes and helping prepare and cook food. Nazma used her mother tongue, Pahari, with all her family. She understood the English used by school-age children, but did not use English to the same level. The older children in Nazma's family attended Qur'anic classes after school. All members of the family recited verses and prayers in Arabic, and read the Arabic primers and the Qur'an at home.

Nazma's mother

During an interview in Nazma's home, her mother and grandmother recalled childhood memories in Azad Kashmir, for example, making their own little kitchen outside the house and playing with clay models:

> At home it's completely different for children – here school is better, but home life is more restricted.

Her mother has high aspirations for her daughter:

> Nazma is quite clever; she does what she is told, follows what she is asked to do and is brighter than the others.

Nazma's mother did not herself speak Urdu, but she wanted her children to do so; all her children spoke Pahari fluently, and she was proud of that. It was her explicit aspiration that all her children should grow up speaking English and Pahari – there was no argument in her mind but that bilingualism is an advantage.

Her mother commented that every morning Nazma became upset about going to school. Being very attached to her mother, she liked staying at home with her. She said:

> I don't know about school, but the teachers know how to help my daughter.

Nazma watched, helped and talked while her mother was preparing and cooking food. Both her grandmother and mother told her their stories from childhood, drawing on an oral tradition which had no written form. Nazma heard her older siblings talking in English and saw the school reading books they brought home. She watched them preparing for Qur'anic classes, reciting verses in Arabic after school and saw the Arabic primers and the Qur'an read by all the older members of the family. From the family's perspective, Nazma's mother had high aspirations for her daughter and wanted her to achieve well in the education system. She had little understanding of how children learn by play at nursery and she relied entirely on the idea that school would give Nazma all the educational skills she required.

The school itself expected parents to understand and respond to its communications, support what it was trying to achieve in the curriculum and assist their children's learning at home. From the school's point of view, Nazma's mother was unable to communicate in English and, although Nazma was the sixth child in the family to attend the nursery, she was not seen as being supported in her school learning at home.

The difficulties that Nazma and her siblings experienced at school were explained away in terms of cultural and language difficulties. Had the nursery staff recognised the value of drawing on Nazma's prior knowledge, however, there would have been some aspects of her home experience that matched well with aspects of the nursery learning, for example her participation in role play and dressing-up activities with siblings at home.

Samia at home

Samia was the middle child of three. She lived with her mother, grandmother and brothers. Her father, a Pahari speaker and a shopkeeper, also shared their home, although he had a new family in Watford. Samia's father came to Watford when he was 9 years old. He had some schooling in England and some in Azad Kashmir, but no qualifications. He spoke, read and wrote both Urdu and English. Samia's mother had attended primary school in Azad Kashmir, but never completed her schooling. She married in Azad Kashmir and came to Watford with her husband. She spoke Pahari but little English or Urdu. Samia's older brother was also born in Azad Kashmir, but Samia and her younger brother, Sadaqat, were both born in Watford.

Samia spoke Pahari with her younger brother, mother and grandmother, while her elder brother spoke some English at home. The recognised community language is Urdu and Samia had started to attend Qur'anic classes after school, where she would learn the Arabic required for reading and reciting the holy text. Her mother was keen to teach her Pahari at home, and tried to nurture the home culture. Samia had no formal pre-school experience in the UK but she had taken a six month holiday in Azad Kashmir with her grandmother before she started school. Her grandmother reported that what Samia had valued most was the space there was for free play. Samia had followed the animals around and played intensively with her cousins and other children in the village. Back in England, she had frequently said 'Let's go back'.

Samia's mother

Samia's mother and grandmother, both present at the interview, were particularly vocal and clear in their views on the education of children and the differing roles of schools and families. Her mother's view was that there is a clear separation between the roles of the home and the school. Only the home can teach the mother tongue, and that is what it should do. It is only when children went to school that they needed to learn English – to teach was the school's role. The home could provide the cultural – and, by implication, linguistic – nurturing that a child needs in the early years. That this excluded

English need not be a problem, as it could easily be acquired later. Samia's mother believed she was doing well at school:

> Samia is an intelligent girl. She is learning very quickly. I hope she will do well, providing she gets enough help, because I cannot help her.

Samia's grandmother shared these views. She saw herself as an uneducated woman, yet she fully understood the importance of education. She tried to help her grandchildren by spending time with them and supporting them morally. She and her daughter missed Azad Kashmir, but appreciated the advantages of a UK education. Nonetheless, she saw how the children missed the open spaces and freedom that Azad Kashmir was able to offer.

Maria at home

Maria was the eldest child of two. She lived with her extended family: both sets of grandparents, who lived next door to each other, parents, cousins, aunts, uncles and her younger brother. Two of her aunts went to school in Watford and her uncles were still at school and doing well. The family had lived in Watford for seven years. Maria's father had lived in Azad Kashmir as a boy and arrived in England as a teenager. He had not attended school, but went to evening classes to learn English. He now works in a factory in North Watford.

Maria understood Urdu but spoke Pahari to her grandparents, parents and younger cousins and sibling. All the children were fluent in Pahari. Her aunts and uncles used English in the home and Maria would try and join in. Her mother commented about her language use:

> She is fine – she tries to speak any language.

Maria did not yet attend Qur'anic classes, but her mother said that she would copy the adults, covering her head while trying to read the Qur'an. Maria had not attended playgroup but her early socialisation in the home was playing with her cousins and younger brother. Her mother commented:

> She is happy playing by herself and her cousins and her little brother at home. She tries to be the leader as she is the elder sister. She sings songs and plays in her own little world.

The family had strong links with Azad Kashmir. Maria stayed there for six months with her family before starting nursery, and her father still visited Azad Kashmir regularly. Her mother talked about Maria's experiences in Azad Kashmir:

> We used to take Maria with us [the women] to the lake near the village to wash the clothes. Maria has seen the river Jhelum and she has been in the water.

Maria's mother

During the interviews, Maria's mother shared childhood memories of growing up in the Kotli area of Azad Kashmir:

> We used to find five or six stones, throw them up in the air and play 'pung gitra' (five stones). We made little rag dolls with long, long hair out of left over cloth and thread with my grandmother. A tailor would visit our home to make clothes and the children used the cuttings and folded the pieces of cloth into matchboxes. We also modelled with clay and dough.

Maria's mother had high expectations for her daughter and expressed her wish for Maria to become a doctor. She also spoke of maintaining cultural and religious values:

> Providing my daughter keeps her cultural and religious values, I will not stop her from achieving this aspiration. She's only four and she's got these high thoughts of herself.

However, she was aware of the possible difficulties in maintaining these values when Maria was older and predicted that her daughter would spend ten to fifteen years in England, to complete her education, and then 'return' to Pakistan.

The children's home experiences

The parental background of the children showed significant similarities. These facts related to circumstances of immigration: all the families originated in the Kotli district of Azad Kashmir, north of Rawalpindi, and all the fathers had emigrated to the UK alone, and had few qualifications. They had settled in Watford, and stayed there. The mothers arrived later, in order to marry, and with only their primary education complete. None of the parents had had any formal pre-school experience.

There were also many similarities in what the parents sought for their children. The youthfulness of the families was noticeable in two cases, the siblings and aunts and uncles of the children were themselves still in full-time education; Nazma's sister had attended a local FE college, while Maria's aunts and uncles were studying for GCSEs at school. Without exception, every mother had high aspirations for her children. Maria's mother was the most specific, wanting her to become a doctor, and the remaining mothers also believed not only that their daughters had the capacity to achieve highly but also that they would do so within the state educational system.

A second common feature was a parallel aspiration: that their daughters would retain and develop their first language and culture. All the children spoke Pahari at home, with parents, grandparents and siblings. The mother tongue was decidedly the main language of communication, and this was not just an inclination but a conscious choice. Samia had already started Urdu language classes, as would the other two children in due course.

However, despite these similarities in the children's home and nursery experiences, there were clear individual differences in the way the three girls experienced early schooling. Most significantly, we see Nazma underachieving in her early schooling whereas by the end of Key Stage One, Samia and Maria do relatively well. These differences are explored in depth through the Inner Layer analysis set out in Chapters 5 and 6.

Summary: introducing Nazma, Samia and Maria

This chapter has set the context for Nazma, Samia and Maria's learning as they entered the English educational system. The children's mothers had high aspirations for their daughters but could not help with their school learning. However, we see in Chapter 3 how the children's teachers were working within a context of inadequate official guidance for practitioners supporting young children learning English as an additional language and, at the same time, a Government agenda of target setting based on nursery Baseline Assessment data.

This situation exposes a vacuum in policy thinking and an overall lack of understanding of the children's situation, and thus presents a considerable challenge to the teachers of Nazma, Samia, and Maria as the girls entered the schooling system and set about learning in English.

Chapters 5 and 6 explore how the children themselves experienced early schooling and discuss the inner layer of analysis. How do Maria, Samia and Nazma find their own way through nursery and what are their individual strategies for getting by and, beyond that, learning during their first year of formal schooling? How did they syncretise home and school learning?

The next chapter considers the process of being a researcher within the context of this study, and discovers ways of understanding young bilingual children's learning at home and at nursery.

2

Multilingual methodologies:
listening to young bilingual children

Maria:	*If I say what I want to be, then the English teachers won't understand*
Grandfather:	*No, they want you to talk in your language*
Maria:	*If I speak my language, they won't understand*
Grandfather:	*It doesn't matter*

[audio recording in mother tongue (Pahari) at Maria's home during her first term at nursery]

This chapter outlines the processes involved in researching young bilingual children's learning that led to this book. The ethnographic approaches to listening, understanding and responding to young bilingual children's voices contributes to the growing body of research that moves and extends beyond listening to predominantly monolingual children. Clark's (2001 and 2005) Mosaic Approach uses interactive, participatory techniques which can lead to rich, illuminating data which represent the child's perspective. The importance of listening to children is central to this approach. Listening is not a matter of 'hearing words' but about listening to all communications, including the non-verbal, which can help us understand children better.

How children are acknowledged by teachers in the classroom relates to the way children communicate. Their 'voice' is established through the ways they communicate, including through spoken exchanges at any given moment and over time. If this is not established because, as in the case of children who still cannot learn English as an additional language, they are as yet unable to engage in spoken exchanges in English, they may be viewed as not having a 'voice' by practitioners, as 'silent' and, since 'voice' registers presence, even as 'invisible'. A commonly held view is that 'the range of language spoken other than English is the most obvious barrier to listening' (Clark and Moss, 2001:51). However, if conventional practice can be extended so that the voices of the bilingual children can be heard, providing insights into the innate strengths they bring to their engagement with learning, a more constructive perspective can be established.

Rather than viewing bilingual children's linguistic diversity as a 'barrier to listening' and so presenting potential difficulties, developing a range of 'multilingual' methodologies can construct wider windows on their learning and deepen our understanding about it. The ethnographic methodologies outlined in this chapter were designed specifically to capture the children's multilingual voices at home and at school. The process of learning through ethnography is presented in some detail, to show how *listening to young children* can include these voices.

Learning through ethnography: the role of the researcher
So what do young bilingual children experience as they start formal schooling? I needed to collect and analyse data in ways that would highlight the rich context of the children's experience and offer new insights and thus the opportunity to interpret data from a different perspective, through different lenses. My essential concern was to give the children and their families an audible voice throughout the study, but not to focus too narrowly on the specific linguistic features of second language acquisition. As someone who did not share the language or culture of the children, I embarked on a fascinating journey of discovery. Consequently, my choice of methodological approach was based on naturalistic investigations of people, their behaviour and perspectives.

An ethnographic approach to studies has made an important contribution to research in the early years (for example, Pollard with Filer, 1996; Connolly, 1998; Thompson, 1999). As MacNaughton, Rolfe, and Siraj-Blatchford (2001) observe:

> the qualitative studies that are currently being applied in early childhood education are also important in allowing new voices to be heard – these are the voices of teachers, other carers, families and the children themselves. (2001:194)

Ethnography as a methodology affords insights into children's learning in a range of contexts. Aubrey *et al* (2000) discuss ways in which ethnography can be empowering for members of the observed community:

> Ethnography aims to help the researchers (*the outsiders*) and others who are not members of the observed community, to understand the group's values, culture and social activities better but also and importantly, ethnography also aims to help the group (*the insiders*) understand themselves and their way of life better. (2000:112)

Griffiths (1998), however, points to the ethical issues for researchers undertaking research for social justice. These are discussed in relation to undertaking research 'on/for/with' (p:40) groups of people and the potential for deception which may arise from doing research as an 'insider but outsider'. She states:

> to the extent that the researchers are insiders, they are drawing on the normal ground rules of reciprocity and trust that pertain for social interactions in the community. To the extent that being a researcher means using these ground rules for research purposes, there is a risk of exploitation and betrayal. (1998:41)

The dilemmas raised here, particularly in relation to trust and reciprocity, were central to the ways in which I designed and carried out my study. I was reminded of my professional role as Pre-school Project Co-ordinator of a team of bilingual outreach assistants, working with minority ethnic parents and their children in the community and school context, and of my commitment to working with the families (the '*insiders*') and the importance of *giving back* to that community. As a white teacher-researcher I was aware of the fine line and subtle differences between 'giving a voice' to the subjects and betraying them' Griffiths (1998:41). Minimising the impact of a researcher's presence in the nursery classroom and, more significantly in the children's homes, was the subject of much discussion during the development stages of the study. However, the strength of relationships I established with teachers, parents, children and community outreach assistants, coupled with the sensitive and open manner in which we worked together, created a sound, ethical basis for the study.

In his discussion of validity in ethnographic studies, Spindler underlines the significance of 'prolonged, intimate contact with, observation of, and inquiry about repetitive patterns of behaviour and interaction' (1982:17).

The need to understand invisible learning, by capturing the voices of bilingual children through the process of repetitive and prolonged inquiry, was the central purpose of my study.

The Research Context table overleaf details the contextual information already noted about the children, the community to which they belong, the

RESEARCH CONTEXT

Child	Mother tongue	Family position	nursery	Age starting Nursery	Community language class	Recordings in nursery	Recordings at home	Interviews
Nazma	Pahari	Youngest of 6 Grandmother lives at home	Circle Nursery Watford	3:6 4 terms in nursery	no	15 hrs total	6 hrs total	2 with teacher 2 with mother
Maria	Pahari	Eldest of 2 Grandparents (4), cousins, aunts, uncles live at home	Ashfield Nursery Watford	4:0 3 terms in nursery	no	15 hrs total	6 hrs total	2 with teacher 2 with mother
Samia	Pahari	Middle child of 3 Grandmother lives at home	Lucca Harris Nursery Watford	4:4 2 terms in nursery	Attends local Qur'anic/ Urdu class	15 hrs total	6 hrs total	2 with teacher 2 with mother

area in which they live and the schools they attended. Nazma, Samia and Maria were all born in Watford, Hertfordshire. The largest minority ethnic community in Watford is Azad Kashmiri. Most families (including those of these children) originate from Azad Kashmir, which borders North-East Pakistan. Their mother tongue is Pahari, a dialect of Punjabi spoken there. Literally 'hill language', it is spoken in the mountainous region and has many regional varieties. Many of the children from Azad Kashmiri backgrounds enter the schooling system with little or no expressive English, including those in this study.

The early socialisation of the three study children was centred at home with their parents, grandparents and other members of their extended family. None had attended playgroup or any pre-school setting in this country. They attended different – but similar – primary schools. In all three, the nurseries are located in a separate building from the primary school. All are multi-ethnic schools, with between 20 per cent and 35 per cent of children from Azad Kashmiri backgrounds. The nursery staff – one nursery teacher and two nursery nurses in each nursery – are all monolingual English speakers and do not share the first languages of their bilingual pupils. Without exception, all were experienced nursery practitioners, who had worked with bilingual children and their families in the same multi-ethnic school for most of their professional lives.

Working in the community
Working with Mussarat: a key actor in the study
Hammersley and Atkinson (1983) discuss the complexities involved in gaining access to the research site and establishing and maintaining relationships with others in the field over the period of ethnographic research. This is a particularly challenging issue for a white monolingual researcher working in the homes of bilingual children. However, close working relationships were established with the bilingual outreach assistants during the Pre-school Community-based Project, and these gave me access to the children's homes and enabled insights into the perspectives of families and the work of bilingual professionals working in their homes. I needed first to establish trust and openness with the families and with my colleagues, and to share an understanding of how this innovative project might evolve.

An ethnographic approach is a commitment to understanding another way of life from the native, or emic, point of view. I sought to achieve this by 'looking for an informant to teach [me] the culture' (Spradley and McCurdy, 1990: 18). I was particularly aware that I needed to acknowledge the understanding of perspectives other than my own and that I too was the learner in this research. My relationship with one of the pre-school outreach assistants, Mussarat, became particularly significant, as she became my mediator of cultural practices and language. She was the most experienced member of the research team and a well respected member of the community. She herself had spent her childhood in Azad Kashmir and had moved to Watford when she married. She had trained as a primary school teacher in Pakistan and, after raising her own children at home, had returned to working with children in school as a bilingual classroom assistant (BCA) in Watford.

We had worked together in one of the study schools and accompanied each other on home visits. Her empathy with families in the community and her ability to interpret the mothers' understandings and perspectives was impressive. As a key actor, she was fundamental to the success of this work. This was the beginning of a long professional relationship and close friendship with Mussarat, during which we discovered and shared many insights into the experiences of children in nursery. The title of Mussarat as a 'key actor' (Fetterman, 1989) appears appropriate here; 'this individual becomes a key actor in the theatre of ethnographic research and plays a pivotal role, linking the fieldworker and the community.' (1989:58).

Working in schools
Three multi-ethnic nurseries
Negotiating access to the classrooms of the three study schools was made easy by my professional role at the time. I had good relationships with the headteachers, who gave permission and support for me to do research in their schools. The nursery teachers, with whom I had previously worked, all welcomed my participation and observation in the classroom. It was agreed that nursery teachers would participate in both formal and informal discussions and that participation would be during the first and final term at nursery. Cumulative records were made of each child's achievements, together with their Baseline Assessment scores. A framework to the background fieldwork was firmly in place.

Selecting the sample: the individual cases of Nazma, Maria and Samia
It was agreed that in order to build the fullest possible description of a bilingual child's early experience of schooling, only a small number of cases would be appropriate.

During our visits to the children's homes, I was struck by the willingness of the mothers to talk about their expectations of school and aspirations for their children. The importance of the mother tongue at home and the central role of the family in its development was a key theme to emerge. This helped determine who should be selected. Selection was based on two principles:

- that development of the children's mother tongue to date should be appropriate for their age
- that parents showed willingness to participate in the study.

Based on these criteria, three girls were selected. Factors relating to sex, age and position in family were also taken into consideration. The girls shared the same mother tongue. Their families originated from Azad Kashmir and now lived in a settled community in Watford. All entered nursery at similar times and transferred to the Reception class in the same school year.

Conduct of the study
Participant observation at nursery
Three sessions were spent in each of the three study nurseries at the beginning of the nursery year, followed by three sessions at the end of the year, though the numbers of recordings per child varied.

I made audio recordings and handwritten field notes for each visit to the nurseries, recording observations of the study child as well as of informal discussions with nursery staff. The field notes were used to contextualise the audio-tape data when I later transcribed the data.

Audio recordings in the nursery
As the study focused on the children's learning of English and use of mother tongue, the method of fieldwork and subsequent analysis of language data were crucial. Audio-recordings were made with a radio-microphone. Each study child carried a light-weight transmitter unit clipped onto a belt, with a radio-transmitter microphone clipped onto her collar. This gave them complete freedom of movement up to a radius of 50 metres, covering the nursery classroom and garden. Each nursery session lasted two and a half hours and the entire teaching session was audio-taped.

On my first visit to each nursery, the BCA was present to introduce me and explain to the study-child the reason why we wanted them to wear the radio-microphone. I had already met them during home visits, but even so they found the experience of wearing a radio-microphone just when they were starting school upsetting at first, especially Samia. During one of the earliest recordings in the nursery, Samia asks the BCA to 'take it off':

[this conversation takes place in Pahari, so is italicised]

Samia: *Teacher, could you take it off?*

BCA: *You don't like it?*

         Now I'll put it higher

Samia: *I want to go to the toilet*

Clearly Samia was worried about going to the toilet while wearing the microphone. The BCA was crucial for Samia's reassurance and her understanding of the recording process. Regular reference to the wearing of radio-microphones was made by other children in the nursery. Such events continued throughout the recording period and not just in the initial stages. The following is typical of the questioning by other children:

[this conversation takes place in English – so is presented in Roman script. These conventions are used throughout the book]

Child A: Why you got that on?

Samia: That one teacher

         You can see that one teacher

However, Maria is more explicit about wearing a radio-microphone:

Child A: Maria, what you done your dress?

Maria: I tape on it

This was evidently a source of fascination to the children, as was my relationship to the study child. Samia replied to one child's questioning about me by saying:

Samia: That's my teacher

         She's coming my house

Observations and audio-recordings in Nazma's home

Key actor Mussarat accompanied me on visits to Nazma's home. Nazma's mother appeared comfortable and the older siblings chatted to me freely after school. However, there were difficulties in the collection of language data. I could make observations of Nazma playing with her siblings or helping her mother at home. But when the radio-microphone was placed on her and the tape recorder switched on, the family appeared to feel obliged to perform for the tape recorder.

To overcome this, we set up the recording equipment as normal, took notes about the context and the family members present and then we left the house while the recording took place (approximately 30-45 minutes). This worked well. During the first few recordings, family members made some references to the recording, and particularly the fact that I had left the house.

In an early recording in Nazma's home she asked her mother:

Nazma: *Where's she gone?*

Why?

During the first home recording in Samia's home, she asked her mother:

Samia: *Why has she left?*

It's slipping [referring to the radio-microphone]

In Nazma's and Samia's homes, no further reference was made to the recording equipment or the process. But in Maria's home, the adults were clearly self-consciousness about the recording process, so tended to direct much of the conversation. An early recording includes the following discussion – in Pahari – of the audience for the tape recordings:

Maria: *If I say what I want to be, then the English teachers won't understand*

Grandfather: *No, they want you to talk in your language*

Maria: *If I speak my language, they won't understand*

Grandfather: *It doesn't matter*

This conversation demonstrates Maria's linguistic awareness, which is advanced for a four-year-old child. She understands early on that her teachers will not understand her language, but her grandfather is aware of the purpose of the research. In a later taping, Maria again demonstrates her understanding of the process:

Grandfather: *You say the things you want to say to your dad – to us*

Ask him for the things you want from Pakistan

Maria: *It's wasting the cassette*

Later on, Mussarat and I listened to and translated the tape together, referring to the contextual notes made beforehand. This took a long time, as the conversations in the home mainly took place in Pahari and needed to be translated and interpreted. The English transcriptions were listed in one column; contextual notes, with Mussarat's comments, observations and interpretations of the data were entered in the other. These observations included per-spectives from Mussarat's personal experience.

Many hours were spent discussing Mussarat's childhood experiences in Azad Kashmir, her knowledge of the families and community and her inside know-ledge of early schooling in Britain. Interestingly, these conversations caused her to reflect on the schooling experience of her own children in Watford, their loss of fluency in Pahari and ultimately their high academic achieve-ments in the system – an increasingly familiar pattern in the losses and gains undergone by bilingual children. It was through these conversations that my awareness of the issues broadened, influencing the direction of the study and its evolutionary process. Mussarat's commentary undoubtedly provided essential insights, informed the analysis of data during the later stages of the study and led to significant interpretations.

Interviews and documentary data

In trying to show how different strands of the children's experience fit to-gether: their mother tongue, their mothers' aspirations for them, their teachers' view of progress, and their competence in English were all explored in the interviews with mothers and teachers.

The interviews with nursery teachers took place in school at the end of the first term. Interviews at home were with the children's mothers – and grand-mothers in some cases – and at the beginning and end of the nursery year.

Interviews at home

Interviews with mothers were conducted by Mussarat in Pahari and were audio-taped. They were designed to combine collecting data about the child and family with establishing rapport with the families and helping them understand our interest in their children's development during the early years of schooling. The conduct of the interviews varied, partly because of the pre-sence of different family members and partly because some questions led to more detailed responses.

Interviews and documentary data at nursery

The nursery teachers were interviewed towards the end of the first term in nursery, after the Nursery Baseline Assessments had been conducted. As well as the teachers' comments on the children's progress, we were given access to the children's Early Years Record of Achievement, Baseline Assessment scores and Key Stage One SAT results. Reception Class teachers and their Year 2 teachers were also interviewed.

We have discussed the conduct of the study in some detail so as to show some of the problems and processes involved in gaining understanding about young bilingual children's invisible learning.

Developing a theoretical framework – from second language acquisition to socio-cultural perspectives

The process of understanding and interpreting the collected data unfolded over nearly a decade. As different forms of data were collected, transcribed and interpreted, I began to speculate about the themes and categories that came to light. It was an extensive process: the data demanded frequent re-visiting, including listening over and over again to the audio-tapes. The conclusion of this process gave rise to new questions which were shared with colleagues in school or with Mussarat.

The framework for analysis was based on evidence of the emerging themes. The nature of my recurring discussions about these key themes related strongly to the notion of the children making their own way as learners. Although I had originally viewed the analysis of data as casting light on the girls' learning of English as an additional language at home and at school, what emerged was a much more complex understanding of the processes involved in learning within a socio-cultural context. How best could my analysis present these complexities of young bilingual children as they learned to learn how to learn during their first year of schooling, and how could my analysis present their *strategic* approach?

Accordingly, I rejected an approach which focused predominantly on an analysis of the children's second language acquisition. Instead I adopted a method of 'multi-layering', using Gregory's (1993) ethnographic approaches. The key themes to emerge related to the difference in the understanding at home and at school of the children's learning and the agency they brought to their situation.

The outer layer of analysis considered early schooling from the teachers' perspective. While the girls were actively engaged in a full family life at home with siblings and extended family, their individual responses to the very different ongoing experience of early schooling was revealed through the observations and recordings of their interactions with others at nursery. This outer layer was one aspect of what is visible or not in the children's learning, since information, views and insights were only minimally shared. Thus, the mothers' view that it would be easy for their daughters to learn English at school, for example, was not known to the nursery teacher and, most importantly, was never the subject of discussion between teacher, parent and child.

Similarly, the teachers' understanding of how the curriculum is planned and delivered, particularly in relation to encouraging independence, was never explicitly shared with the parents.

What does become apparent on closer inspection is the increasing awareness of an inner layer of understanding by the children themselves. I was particularly impressed by the ways in which they found their way through nursery and began to take control.

I saw these responses to their learning as strategic and began to look at the inner layer of data in terms of their strategies. By 'strategy' I mean the ways in which the girls negotiated different micro contexts, steering their way through the demands and opportunities, depending on how these are presented to and perceived by them. 'Strategy' does not necessarily imply a conscious choice on their part, as there are constraints imposed on them by the early years education system, but it does imply that as an agent of her own learning, the child has a controlling role.

The following transcript of Samia at home provided new insights into the significance of the collected data. Listening to this recording with Mussarat, we were fascinated at having captured such a natural, hidden or invisible view into Samia's learning. Mussarat commented at the time that she had not realised that Samia could use so much school language and that at times she sounded just like her nursery teacher.

It is clear from the beginning of the next transcript that Samia and her brother Sadaqat (aged 2) were totally unaware of the microphone clipped onto Samia's collar. At the time (1.30 pm) their mother was in the kitchen and the siblings were upstairs. Samia has entered into her role in the 'school game' she was enacting. She started by inviting her brother into her game, using Pahari:

Samia and Sadaqat play school transcript

1 Samia: Little bit

Things back

Little bit back

That not school [to Sadaqat]

5   *Come in school, Sadaqat*

Come in school

Over the first three lines Samia is repeating a short phrase, which leads to a variation or extension. Given greater freedom to experiment in the play situation, and in the familiar context of her home, Samia's language in the transcript below goes on to show a wider range of lexis, structures and knowledge of English than is apparent when she is at school. She is clearly rehearsing the language heard at nursery, repeating chunks or formulaic phrases of familiar situations.

We also have insights into Samia's mother tongue, which she uses with fluency in her interactions with Sadaqat.

1. Samia: *Sadaqat, stand up*

                We're not having group time *now*

                Group time

Here we recognise the routines of nursery in her play. For example, she refers to a key aspect of the High/Scope routine, which involves 'having group time'. Much of her English language use relates to that used by adults to children in nursery routines. It also reflects the language of instruction. For example, later in the recording, Samia gives a series of instructions to her little brother:

                You can play, Sadaqat

5.   *Shall we play something?*

                You want to do painting?

                [noise from Sadaqat]

                OK get your water

                Let's get a water

10.   Let's get a water

                Let's get a paper

                Baby didn't cry

                Hurry up (whispering)

                You want paper

15.   And put in the painting

                Do that and what are you choose colour

                Black

Sadaqat: Back

20.Samia:	No, there's a black
	Did you finish it?
	Painting
	You make it
	Sadaqat, do it with this finger
25.	*Do it like this, do it like that*
	Wash
	Which colour *are you going to choose*
	Next thing
	Don't do it, Sadaqat
30.	*Orange satsuma*
	I'm doing it satsuma colour

When Samia wants to draw Sadaqat into the game or when she wants to give him a real instruction, one that she wants her brother to follow, she uses Pahari. There is, therefore, a distinction within the game, which is on the one hand the 'school game' in English, and on the other what she needs her brother to do to make the game work, requiring the use of Pahari. But there are times when the distinction between engaging her brother to enable the game to work and her use of English to play the school game breaks down and Pahari is spoken instead of English (*'I'm doing it satsuma colour'*). This merging of purpose is reflected in the code-switching and code-mixing (*'what* colour *are you going to choose?'*). Samia code-switches into Pahari to keep Sadaqat engaged in the game (*'Sadaqat, do it with this finger'*). There is a recognisably smooth transition between the two languages and the same lexis is used in both mother tongue and English during the conversation, for example, painting, colour, satsuma (orange).

	(clapping, knocking)
	You are having your...
	(crying)
35.	Like it?
Sadaqat:	*Mummy* [calling to mother]
Samia	*Let's do some painting*
	Do it like this, Sadaqat

Red

40. *Don't do it*

Now you can do it

Now we've done it

Finish

I have

45. *Sadaqat, put it over there*

And let's do some painting

Wash up

Sadaqat, give it to big sister

Give paper and I'll do wash up

Put paper over there

Now it's story time

Samia's home play with her brother reveals the extent to which she has absorbed everyday language used by adults at the nursery. This displays her remarkable but invisible capacity to use linguistic skills within a role play, a situation entirely managed on her own terms, satisfying her need to practise or rehearse her English, and in effect vicariously taking on and completing the routine school tasks. It becomes a private, personal achievement, spoken in English, whilst at the same time recognising the need for an additional linguistic role, spoken in Pahari, to control and share the game with her brother. This contrasts sharply with the language she learns through social interaction with her peers at nursery. It also shows how successfully she has absorbed school routines and, for her, the demanding expectations of the nursery setting. Cultural learning of this kind is very important in developing her confidence in learning what to do and how to behave, and is closely interwoven with her language learning.

Her use of the language of adults in her role play illustrates how her language learning and her developing socio-cultural positioning is related to taking on the voice of influential others. In lines 17-19 of this excerpt, we see the synergy or unique reciprocity whereby an older child teaches her younger sibling while at the same time developing her own learning. This is also demonstrated by how she code-switches to include Sadaqat in her role play (see lines 4-6 for example). Throughout her school game with her younger brother

Samia is scaffolding her own learning and demonstrating an understanding of early schooling that has previously been invisible to the educators of young bilingual children.

A key insight into young bilingual children's learning is shown in her play at home with a younger brother: it reveals not only how school learning flows over into play at home, but also how Samia takes control of her learning herself. She becomes the key player in the learning process. She manages the play with her brother so as to engage him and to reinforce her own language learning in addition to learning acquired through the nursery curriculum. Again, much of the developmental process Samia demonstrates is not visible to the nursery teacher. The skills she shows in play with her brother, her use of English, her facility for code-switching, her ability to engage, sustain and direct her younger brother's involvement, her manipulation of school knowledge (for example, colours), are manifest, but their invisibility means they are not known to, or understood by, her nursery teacher.

Summary: multilingual methodologies

The discussion about multilingual methodologies highlights my professional roles and relationships with the families, the community members and school staff. The sense of a shared concern to understand Nazma, Samia and Maria's early learning and the desire to establish a meaningful authenticity to the study underpinned the methodological approach:

- ■ 'capturing' children's voices using ethnographic approaches
- ■ establishing relationships based on trust and reciprocity with colleagues and the families
- ■ working with a mediator – key actor – of matching culture and language throughout the study
- ■ collecting data using a range of lenses – observations, interviews, audio-recordings, documentary evidence – within different contexts – at home and in nursery, with adults and with children
- ■ repeatedly listening to and discussing the meaning behind children's invisible learning.

In the next chapter we study the context for the learning of Nazma, Samia and Maria in the nursery and explore the learning experiences which are visible to the nursery teachers.

3

Visible learning at nursery

Nazma enters nursery

Nazma enters nursery holding her sister's hand. Her sister, Yasmin (aged four and a half), moves over to the large carpet where the children sit with the nursery teacher at the beginning of every session. Nazma follows her, chewing her dress, staying close to her sister and watching everything. She had stopped crying during the fifth week at nursery and she now comes every afternoon. The children listen to the teacher talking about caterpillars and many join in the discussion in English. Nazma is silent. Mussarat, the Bilingual Classroom Assistant, enters the nursery. She gathers a small group of Pahari speaking children together to share a book. This activity had been planned with the nursery teacher and linked to the current topic. The children switch to Pahari (their mother tongue) for this activity. Nazma listens and points to a picture of a dog (*kutha*) and cat (*billee*) in an Urdu alphabet picture book, but does not speak. They go outside to play. Nazma stands on the outside watching the other children and holds Mussarat's hand. She has learned the climbing frame routine and repeats the climbing and sliding activity several times. The children go inside and choose from a range of play activities. Nazma watches. She stays at an activity for one minute and moves on. This is repeated several times. Then she wanders around the room sucking her fingers. It is now story time on the carpet. The children sit and listen to the story of *The Very Hungry Caterpillar*. Nazma sits close to her sister and watches. Their mother appears at the door and they go home. [Drury, 1997]

Nazma is less than four years old and she has attended nursery for seven weeks. This picture represents her visible learning in the context of an English nursery class. But what can we understand about her invisible learning? How can we capture her silent voice as she begins the task of learning in school and at home? And how can we represent her many languages?

I n this chapter the Outer Layer or the nursery context for young bilingual children's early schooling is explored. The three children whose stories are the subject of this book are introduced, along with the context for them as they enter the English educational system. It begins with a snapshot or vignette of each child as they begin to engage in their early learning experience in nursery, the children's visible learning as seen by their nursery teachers. Each child's position as a developing bilingual learner is described against the background of the national goals for learning. The teachers' views of the children's overall development is discussed, including the contribution they think each family makes to their pupil's learning. The children's Nursery Baseline Assessment scores and ongoing teacher assessments of their progress during their nursery education are taken into account. Evidence is presented of their progress during their first term in Reception, based on an interview with their Reception classteacher and the Infant Baseline Assessment scores, in addition to their Key Stage One SAT results. The views of their classteachers in Year 2 are also presented. Their teachers' views are set within the context of current policy in respect of young children for whom English is an additional language and they serve to introduce the nursery settings.

Nazma, Maria and Samia's nursery teachers are all experienced practitioners who have worked in multi-ethnic nurseries for most of their teaching careers. But what guidance will they find in official policy documents?

The Early Years Context: Policy
The recent emphasis on inclusion of all children in mainstream classrooms has led to more frequent references to children learning English as an additional language (or EAL). In England, the principles for early years education were set out in the Curriculum Guidance for the Foundation Stage (QCA, 2000). It aimed to 'foster personal, social and emotional well-being' through 'promoting an inclusive ethos and providing opportunities for each child to become a valued member of that group and community so that a strong self-image and self-esteem are promoted.' This statement, like the other aims for early learning at the Foundation Stage, might have been seen in the light of the government's intention for education to be 'inclusive' and to promote equality of opportunity. The phrase 'each child' therefore included children from all social and cultural backgrounds, 'different ethnic groups' and 'diverse linguistic backgrounds'.

The requirements of the curriculum to ensure equality of opportunity and to make provision for children learning English as an additional language are crucial, but early childhood educators, the teachers of Nazma, Samia and

Maria, need to know what features of good practice, or what principles, will provide a framework to help them to meet the needs of bilingual children. These are not explicit in current, official documentation. Furthermore, there have been few studies in this country which examine the practical implications of the principles that have been promoted. For example, ways in which monolingual nursery staff take advantage of 'building on children's home experience' (in cases of children from homes in which little English is spoken) have not been addressed. As children begin their formal schooling, the interface between the contexts of nursery education, the home and the wider community is closer than at any other stage of education. Equality of opportunity therefore has particular significance for nursery staff.

The development of English as an additional language has received little attention in the UK. There may be several reasons – one could be the widespread view that young bilingual children will quickly pick up English by osmosis simply by being in an active learning environment.

'If the language environment is natural, consistent and stimulating, children will pick up whatever languages are around' (Crystal, 1987). In the 1980s, much emphasis was placed on the importance of a stress-free environment for language learning (Krashen, 1985). However, this was often interpreted as meaning that learning English as an additional language is a natural process. Although it is widely believed that the early years environment is an ideal setting for capitalising on young children's natural ability to pick up English, studies have shown that the language learning situation of bilingual children is far more complex than is generally recognised. This may be because few contributors to official documents have expertise in teaching bilingual children or cannot draw on such expertise. There have been relatively few research studies to inform policy makers and practitioners about the strategies that will best assist children learning EAL in the early years.

What contribution can the stories of Nazma, Samia, Maria make to our understanding of young bilingual children's early learning? As the learning environment they first enter is determined by current policy and the knowledge, understanding and training of their nursery teachers, we must look carefully at what happens to them when they begin nursery and how their teachers view them and their experience of schooling.

Nazma at Circle nursery

The vignette of Nazma at the beginning of this chapter is a snapshot of her experience as she enters nursery after attending for seven weeks. She stopped crying during the fifth week at nursery and she was then coming every after-noon. During her early days in the nursery, none of the monolingual nursery staff engaged with Nazma except for classroom management purposes, and there was little verbal interaction between her and other children in the nursery, apart from her sister who was in the same group. She was, however, able to understand and communicate with the BCA.

Nazma's early home socialisation has taken place in her mother tongue. So when she first entered nursery, she met an abrupt change of both language and cultural expectations. In an English language environment, she was in effect dispossessed of her ability to communicate and the impact of this on a three or four year old can be profoundly disturbing. Indeed, if Nazma happened to attend a session when the BCA was not there, she was left largely to her own devices. Nazma's limited engagement at this time may have been caused not only by her inability to use English but also because of the mismatch between her home experiences and those of the nursery.

Circle nursery was in a large Victorian building, across the playground from the main school. The room adjoined the Reception class and a spacious hall-way divided the two classes; this area comprised the early years unit. The main areas of learning in the nursery class were clearly set out: an imaginative play area, set up as a home corner, a book corner, a painting/drawing/ sticking area, a writing table, a large carpeted area and tables for construction/ imaginative play, a computer area, and sand and water. There were about 30 children at the afternoon session of nursery which Nazma attended for two and a half hours a day. The nursery teacher worked with two nursery nurses and a part-time bilingual classroom assistant and she was experienced at working in multi-ethnic early years classrooms. Each adult in the nursery was responsible for her own small group of children. When they first arrived in the morning, the children worked with their key adult and participated in their group's activity. Then they chose from the range of play activities set out. Approximately halfway through the session, they went outside and played with the equipment on the paved area outside the nursery. It was then drink time, followed by further play activities. The session ended with a story and songs in a whole group on the carpet.

Nazma's Nursery teacher – Miranda
Nazma started Circle nursery when she was 3 years 6 months old and spent four terms there. Her teacher, Miranda, reported that Nazma was very upset during her first weeks in nursery. At the beginning of her first term Miranda wrote in her anecdotal notes about Nazma:

Came in normal time, instead of later; cried, wouldn't settle for about an hour or so; just sobbed and sucked fingers and had cuddles; stopped crying for a bit, then had a chuckle.

As a result it was agreed with her mother that during the first term she should attend nursery only twice weekly, when the BCA, Mussarat was there. There was no Nursery Baseline Assessment in place during Nazma's first term. But Miranda wrote in her report at the end of Nazma's final term:

Nazma is extremely reluctant to communicate in English. She understands most instructions given to her but obstinately refuses to say anything. Occasionally, she will say a whole sentence but soon becomes silent again. She communicates with other Asian children in her home language. She enjoys playing in the home corner and can be quite assertive. Nazma knows and recognises basic colours in English. She can name a circle shape. During collaborative reading sessions Nazma is often distracted. She will sometimes point to the text but will not say anything. She recognises eight out of 13 children's name cards in her group. Nazma is recalcitrant about joining in with PE sessions.

When interviewed, her teacher commented on Nazma's self-sufficient and stubborn personality: 'She is refusing to speak, knowing it is required of her... I expected her to verbalise more, language is taking a long time to come out.' In terms of her language development, there was an understanding of the difficulty of the task facing Nazma when she started nursery: 'It was a strange place, with people speaking a foreign language.' She added, 'she's saying: I know you want me to speak and I'm not going to.'

Despite these observations Miranda commented on how Nazma 'came to life' with the BCA, and she saw mother tongue support as crucial for Nazma's personal, social, emotional and language development. So why did she regard Nazma as stubborn, reluctant, recalcitrant?

Nazma's Reception classteacher

Infant Baseline Assessment was carried out during the first few weeks in Reception and Nazma scored 23 out of a possible score of 51. In the box labelled 'Areas of significant concern' the teacher wrote, 'hardly ever speaks unless she wants something'. She scored 3 out of a possible 12 for Language and Listening Experience and the lowest possible scores for Social and Emotional and Approaches to Learning. After four terms in nursery, these scores represented a significant challenge for the school. In an interview with the Reception class teacher during her first term, she commented on Nazma's approach to learning:

> Nazma is not keen to learn things. She doesn't do what you ask her, she ignores instructions. She is not good at counting. She won't do the work. It's her personality. Sometimes she refuses to do things.

However, the central concern of her classteacher was Nazma's silence:

> When she speaks, she can speak a sentence. But she doesn't speak much. She has stopped talking to me. She doesn't appear to listen. She doesn't look at the teacher. Is she pretending?

Her teacher realised that Nazma would require special support. She suggested possible strategies to help her: giving her a lot of time, one-to-one work and shared reading. She was familiar with Nazma's siblings and compared their early schooling experiences:

> She is brighter than Yasmin, more able. Hasnan was quiet, but didn't refuse to speak. She is silent at register. I am hoping that one day she will speak.

Nazma's Year 2 classteacher

During the interview with her Year 2 classteacher, it became evident that Nazma had had a breakthrough during the last term in Key Stage One. Her teacher expressed this in terms of her showing greater confidence conversing with peers in English, although she was 'only just speaking in class'. However, her end of Key Stage One SATs results reflected how Nazma was struggling with the demands of the National Curriculum. She scored Level One in all subjects, indicating that she was under-achieving in all areas. But her classteacher was clear that 'She does not have a learning difficulty. She is average for a bilingual child. She makes herself understood'.

Subject	NC Level
Mathematics	1
Speaking and listening	1
Reading	1
Writing	1
Reading Comprehension	1

Her teacher observed that Nazma was 'very tolerant, pleasant, friendly and extremely motivated'. She went on to reflect more generally on bilingual children's learning in school:

> They need time for a solid foundation to be established. It is important never to push them to be verbal. If they are not ready, you should not force them to speak. There are not enough opportunities for play. They need opportunities to talk and develop their use of language.

Nazma's classteacher told me that no English was spoken in the home so she had learned it at school. She was pleased with Nazma's progress and particularly 'her spirit, motivation, determination and hard work'. She described Nazma as 'chipping away' at her learning of English.

Nazma's classteacher predicted that:

> She'll be fine. She endears herself. However, she needs time and the opportunity to develop at her own pace.

Samia at Lucca Harris nursery

Here is a snapshot of four year old Samia during one session in her first term at nursery.

Samia enters nursery

> Samia enters Lucca Harris nursery holding her mother's hand. She finds her 'giraffe' picture and places it on the planning board. She has planned her work-time in the art and craft area and she stands watching a nursery nurse organising a hand painting activity at the painting table. The children are each making hand printed cards for mother's day. She takes a turn at the activity in silence, except for the correct one word response to questions about the colour of the paint and the card – 'What's that colour?' 'Yellow'. Samia then moves onto the carpet where children are playing with a wooden train set, solid shapes and small construction materials. She is silent while she plays on her own. After a few minutes, another child takes one of her shapes and she protests 'No, mine, not yours. Look.' There is no response and she continues playing. Talk is going on around her, but it is not addressed to Samia. The nursery teacher walks past the carpet and Samia attracts her attention, 'Mrs Ashley, look.' The teacher walks away and it is tidy up time. Samia sits with the teacher in a group of seven children for small group time. The focus is the song 'Heads, shoulders, knees and toes' and playing a game to teach the names of parts of the body. She joins in the refrain of the song 'Knees and toes', listens, watches attentively and participates mainly non-verbally during the game. Then the teacher directs the children: 'It's time to go out in the garden'. She finds Samia sitting on her own singing to herself 'knees and toes, knees and toes', before she goes out to play.

This account indicates Samia's route through the time and space of the nursery setting during one session. There were choices to make, areas to move to, times when playing alone was acceptable and times when participation was required, and there were instructions to understand and carry out. Throughout her first term in nursery, Samia was developing her understanding of the procedural rules (Street and Street, 1993) and expectations of this new social world. For example, she knew the routine at the start of the session in which children were expected to identify 'their' picture and place it on the planning board to show what area or activity they wished to choose. She knew the different areas of the nursery and what they were used for. She knew that it was acceptable to play quietly on her own at certain times but that she would be expected to join in teacher-led group activities.

Haste (1987) observes that 'in acquiring these rules, the child learns a basis for interactions with others, and the shared cultural framework for making sense of the world' (*op.cit.*: 163). During her first term at nursery, Samia had to learn a wide range of rules and routines to do with how time and space were organised in the nursery and the behaviour expected. By the end of her first term she had gone beyond the initial stage of insecurity in a new environment. She now had the confidence to attract the teacher's attention when necessary and to object when shapes she was playing with were taken by other children – 'No, mine. Not yours'. Nevertheless, her limited grasp of English meant that her acculturation in the setting precipitated times of stress and difficulty. The process of adaptation involved a new shaping of her identity as Samia discovered and internalised what is acceptable in the socio-cultural environment. Willett (1995) pointed out that learners acquire more than linguistic rules through interactional routines: 'they also appropriate identities, social relations and ideologies' (*op.cit.*: 477).

The Lucca Harris nursery was situated in a separate building adjacent to the primary school. In its large open plan room, the main areas of learning were set out as follows: art and craft area, construction area, imaginative play area, natural area, book corner, computer area and the outside garden. Approximately 30 children came to the morning session, which Samia attended for two and a half hours a day. Nearly half the children were bilingual and most of these spoke Pahari. The nursery teacher, Kate, worked with two nursery nurses and a part-time bilingual classroom assistant. She knew the families whose children attended her class. The structure and routines of the nursery were particularly significant as it followed a High/Scope approach to the curriculum. This encouraged the children to plan their activities when they first arrived, using a planning board. Children were to do the activity during work time and then to review or recall their learning with their key adult in a small group. In addition to this central 'plan, do, review' routine for each nursery session, there were focused, teacher-directed, small group activities based on the High/Scope 'key experiences' which covered the requirements for the Early Learning Goals set out in the Curriculum Guidance for the Foundation Stage (QCA, 2000). The session ended with all the children outside in the garden and then back for story and singing on the carpet.

Samia's nursery teacher – Kate

Samia began school a term after her fourth birthday and had two terms at nursery. When she started, the nursery teacher, Kate, told her mother, 'If nobody helps her now, she will find it hard to adjust to school'. Kate saw Samia as bright, confident and strong willed. In her Early Years Record of Achievement, she had recorded the following comments for Term 1:

> Samia has settled quietly into Nursery. She uses the planning board to find activities and mostly works alone at painting, jigsaws or sometimes in the imaginative area or construction area.

> Samia didn't speak today – sometimes says one or two words. I gave her some ideas at Recall eg painting and she nodded agreement.

Samia's Nursery Baseline Assessment score was 29 out of a possible score of 41. However, her 'Language Experience' was assessed in mother tongue rather than English – as was the case for Maria – so her overall score was higher. Her score for Social and Emotional approaches to Learning was 12 out of 30 and highlighted the adjustment Samia still needed to make during her early days in nursery.

Kate commented that at times Samia refused to speak and was strong-willed:

> She is bright enough to follow what is going on. She has a definite awkward streak and at times she doesn't do what you want her to do. She can follow activities during work time and engages in a range of activities. She likes puzzles and painting. She is settled, but not chatty, because she missed a term of nursery.

Her nursery teacher also had an understanding of Samia's language development:

> Her mother tongue is strong therefore I would expect her English to come on well too.

But Kate hoped that she would socialise more with her peers, develop greater confidence in English and speak it more. She reported that the BCA worked with Samia in the nursery and supported home-school links. Her family are viewed as supportive and 'keen for Samia to get on'.

Samia's Reception classteacher

Samia's Reception classteacher told me:

> She has adapted well to a more formal classroom. She is, however, strong willed and likes to be in control. She knows the classroom routines well, but she has gaps in her understanding of instructions. Relationships are a problem. She is too strong and has a pushy way. She jumps in when answering questions.

Her teacher viewed Samia's personality as a problem at times. However, her Infant Baseline Assessment scores highlight how well Samia had adapted to school. She achieved a total of 41 out of 51 and her scores for Social and Emotional and Approaches to Learning were particularly impressive after only two terms at nursery: 17 out of 18. Her concentration, motivation and independence achieved the maximum score. Her Language Experience and Mathematical experience score was 16 out of 24. Her teacher commented:

> She achieves what she needs to achieve in English. She can communicate most necessary things through words and phrases. She uses her mother tongue during free play and uses Pahari in her friendship groups. She particularly likes the home corner.

There are clearly aspects of Samia's English language development which her teacher identified as requiring additional support, particularly small group work with well planned activities. In general, Samia had a good first term in Reception.

Samia's Year 2 classteacher

From an interview with her Year 2 classteacher, it is evident that Samia achieved exceptionally well by the end of Key Stage One SATs, scoring above expectations for her age group in English.

SUBJECT	NC Level
Mathematics	2B
Speaking and listening	3
Reading	3
Writing	2B
Reading Comprehension	3

Her classteacher comments positively on her progress and particularly her self-motivation. However, concerns about her personality were still apparent and are summarised in this extract from her end of Year 2 report:

> Her dominant character has resulted in disputes on many occasions. Samia finds it difficult to deal with situations and others when she is not in control and can become very upset.

When asked about home school links, her teacher said there was little contact with the family, although she felt that Samia's learning was supported at home.

In summary, her classteacher viewed her as very able and predicted that:

> She will achieve, she has the potential and knows what she wants to do.

Maria at Ashfield nursery

The following vignette of Maria during one session in her fifth week at nursery provides a composite picture of her experience during her early days at school.

Maria enters nursery

> She finds her place on the carpet alongside the other 28 children in the class. This is her fifth week at school. She cried during her first days but she is quiet now. At the beginning of the morning the teacher introduces the activities for the session to the whole class. It is then small group time and Maria joins a Nursery Nurse for a planning session. In response to being asked three times: 'Maria, what would you like to do?' she says 'painting' and moves over to the hand painting activity table. She paints her hands silently alongside Kiran, and then washes her hands. Then she moves to the dough table and sits with two English speaking girls who are engaged in imaginative play, making cakes. Maria is silent except for one interaction. When asked 'can I have some more cake?' she replies emphatically 'no.' At the cutting activity Maria is making a face, using paper shapes, while a Nursery Nurse interacts with her. She gives one word replies to questions about her face; 'one', 'two', 'nose', 'mouth', 'eye', 'brown'. Maria then moves over to the carpet and plays on her own with wheeled toys and small construction. Then she stands and watches the other children. She sings 'ba ba black sheep' to herself quietly as she plays. It is home time and she is collected by her Auntie at the nursery door.

This vignette of Maria during her fifth week at nursery shows her playing quietly on her own for much of the time during her early stages of English language development. There was no evidence of use of mother tongue in the nursery except when a BCA was present. Although this is contrary to accepted nursery language policy and to QCA Guidance on EAL, it was not a surprising situation given the inadequacy of official guidance referred to earlier in this chapter. Since guidance set out broad principles without engaging with how to achieve them in practice, it tended to have the force of rhetoric rather than firm commitment. One result was that official encouragement for the use of home languages was not always applied in practice.

Maria had learned the nursery routines and procedures and could participate in activities without speaking to other children. But she was missing out by not experiencing the ongoing rich play experiences, in either English or mother tongue. Instead she was supported by a Nursery Nurse and encouraged to contribute to conversations about the painting and dough, for example, using only one word utterances.

Ashfield nursery is situated in a separate building adjacent to a primary school in North Watford. The areas of learning were set out in a large open plan room, to include an imaginative play area, construction area on the carpet, sticking, drawing and painting area, dough table, book corner and outside garden. About 30 children attended the morning session of nursery, which Maria attended for two and a half hours a day. Approximately one quarter of her class were bilingual and four children in addition to Maria spoke Pahari.

The nursery teacher, Lisa, worked with two nursery nurses and a part time BCA. All the staff in Ashfield nursery had considerable experience of working in a multi-ethnic school context. The structure and routines of the nursery followed a child-centred and traditional play-based approach to the curriculum. At the beginning of each session, the children gathered on the carpet to be introduced to the range of activities by an adult, and then chose from the range of learning experiences available for the session. The adults supported the children in specific areas or undertook observations of them. The children were free to move to their chosen activity as they wished for most of the session. During the last half hour, they had a snack and a story or singing session, usually in a small group.

Maria's nursery teacher – Lisa

Maria started nursery when she was four years old. In an interview with Lisa after the first few weeks of Maria's first term in nursery, she told me she considered her to be confident and 'brighter than other bilingual children':

> I knew she was going to achieve. In a small group, she copies and tries to join in. Bilingual children tend to start off shy because they haven't had the same home experiences. Support from home and a strong personality is an advantage for bilingual children at nursery. We try to give them attention and develop the right sort of relationship. It is important you have respect.

However, the nursery nurse noted on her Nursery Progress record for Term 1:

> Maria was cross with everyone for being left at nursery in the early days and cried every day.

Her Nursery Baseline Assessment scores underlined the challenges faced by Maria and the nursery staff during her early days at nursery. She scored 20 out of a possible 41, with significant areas requiring development in Language Experience/Mathematical Experience, where she scored 3 out of 12, and in Approaches to Learning, where she scored 4 out of 9.

The Baseline Assessment takes place during the first seven weeks of a child's first term in nursery and in both parts Maria attained the lowest possible score (i.e. one). In terms of her language development, she 'listens to an adult or child in 1:1 situation' and 'communicates needs non-verbally'. Maria attained similarly low scores in the Independence and Motivation strands of the Approaches to Learning section of the Nursery Baseline Assessment. The comment about her Independence was: 'she often needs adult support/ interaction to engage in a variety of activities and motivation is usually limited to self chosen contexts'.

Yet her nursery teacher saw Maria as coming from a loving home which nurtured confidence, and she had high expectations of her:

> Her strong personality will get her through. She is quick to catch on.

Her Nursery Progress report for the second half of the first term reflected this view:

> Maria has shown herself to be a very determined and intelligent girl, tackling all aspects of nursery with enthusiasm and skill – providing she has chosen the task.

In relation to her language development, Lisa observed that Maria loved stories and was keen to bring her book bag in to nursery. She noted that the BCA worked with her twice a week and said that Maria was keen to learn English and the staff supported her by 'talking to her a lot'. Maria was described as having 'a grown-up and mature attitude to school'. The staff commented that she would initiate conversations with adults and had picked up English from other children in the nursery. Lisa considered that Maria 'will go from strength to strength in the future'.

Maria's Reception classteacher

Maria's Reception classteacher reported that she had settled in well to the Reception class and was beginning to pick up English:

> Maria's language has improved tremendously since the Baseline Assessment. She was very quiet in nursery, but she isn't here. She is very keen to do things. She is reading and picking up sight vocabulary. She speaks in a

large group, putting up her hand to answer questions. She knows her alphabet. She is behind with number work. She finds it difficult to verbalise mathematical language. But she has come on in leaps and bounds and asks a question if she doesn't understand.'

Maria's Infant Baseline Assessment scores reflected the progress she had made. The assessment took place during her first few weeks in the Reception class. She achieved a total of 38 out of a possible 51. Particularly striking was her score of 15 out of 18 for Social and Emotional Approaches to Learning and 9 out of 9 for Physical Skills. Clearly Maria had adapted to school very well indeed and her strong personality, motivation, concentration and independence had added to the teachers' positive view of her as a learner in school. However, her scores in Language experience (English) and Mathematical experience were less successful and reflected the typical position for young bilingual learners developing English language skills – for these areas of learning she scored 14 out of 24.

But at this stage in her school career, her classteacher viewed Maria as:

Keen to learn and join in. Her Auntie comes into school to ask questions and she is doing her homework.

Her progress was viewed as very good and it was anticipated that she would achieve very well at the end of Key Stage One SATs.

Maria's Year 2 classteacher
I returned to the school to interview her Year 2 classteacher after Maria had completed Key Stage One. Her achievements in the end of Key Stage One SATs were very good – her scores were above those expected at this stage in her schooling.

SUBJECT	NC Level
Mathematics	2A
Speaking and listening	2
Reading	2A
Writing	2A
Reading Comprehension	2A

Her Year 2 classteacher commented:

Maria has a good attitude to learning. She is self-motivated to do well, bright and able, top of the bilingual children in her class.

She added that Maria had acted as translator or interpreter for Usman, a child in her class who had recently arrived from Pakistan, and that she was confident and mature in this role. When asked about links between home and school, her teacher said that there had been no contact, apart from parents evenings. However, her Auntie had recently been appointed as a Classroom Assistant in the school. The teacher's views on Maria's future progress were:

> Maria has real potential. She will go far.

Summary: visible learning at nursery

The principles for early years education are set out in the *Curriculum Guidance for the Foundation Stage* document and offer a framework intended to include the needs of bilingual children. For example, the importance of ensuring positive transition from home to school is underlined: 'practitioners should ensure that all children feel included, secure and valued... early years experience should build on what children already know and can do' (QCA, 2000:11) – sound advice which echoes many previous reports (for example, Bullock 1975). However, how this can be achieved for children whose mother tongue and home culture is not English is not addressed and for practitioners working with Nazma, Samia and Maria these principles offer a significant challenge.During her interpretation of the bilingual data Mussarat said that, from her experience of working in early years classrooms,

> The reception of bilingual children when they first enter nursery decides the direction in which they will proceed during their school life. The outgoing, confident children will find their way through, while others will stay inside their shells and not come out for the time they are at school.

Nazma's teacher reported that she was very upset during her first weeks in nursery. She clung to her mother, couldn't settle and didn't speak, except when the BCA was there. In contrast, both Samia and Maria were viewed by their nursery teachers as confident and bright children who coped well with the transition from home to nursery, nursery to school. Samia talked confidently to her friend in Pahari and was beginning to use some English, particularly during small group time: for example, 'I do painting.' Maria was viewed by her nursery teacher as 'brighter than her bilingual peers'.

This study shows that although the education system acknowledges the presence of bilingual children who are learning English as an additional language, their learning paths are not always visible to their early educators. It is the children themselves who are faced with the effects of being unable to communicate in a context they do not yet understand and in which they are not at ease. It is the central role of the child in her own learning, and this is the focus of the second part of this book.

PART TWO

THE ROLE OF THE CHILD
AS A LEARNER

4

Young bilingual learners:
a socio-cultural perspective

Samia: *Sadaqat, stand up*

We're not having group time *now*

Group time

[audio recording of Samia playing school with her two-year old brother at home]

In this chapter I establish the key theoretical frameworks which formed the basis for understanding Nazma, Samia and Maria's learning. Firstly, I discuss a holistic socio-cultural approach to the language and learning development of bilingual children, which is based on the social, cultural and historical approach to cognition provided by Vygotsky. It incorporates and extends a socio-cultural interpretation of agency in the context of early schooling. Secondly, the constructs of scaffolding, guided participation and synergy are used within the socio-cultural perspective to explore and extend aspects of the role of adults, peers and siblings working with young bilingual children in the 'zone of proximal development (ZPD)'. Thirdly, most researchers of bilingual children in the nursery, with the exception of Wong-Fillmore, have focused on language acquisition and social interaction. I examine the process of learning English as interwoven with these other aspects of learning and specifically the silent period.

Theoretical perspectives

We saw in previous chapters how bilingual children starting school have to face the challenges of learning the language and culture they find in the nursery context. These circumstances are predetermined by early years policy, practice and training. A bilingual child's response to the requirement to adapt to the nursery setting involves the interplay between several individual factors inherent in the child and the ways in which early formal schooling is constructed and delivered in the setting. In this sense, the decisions taken by staff are only interpretations of an existing context which has been socially constructed. Just as the nursery staff have individually absorbed what is required by the approved nursery setting so that they can implement it successfully, so the children also come to understand what is acceptable and required.

For bilingual children with limited English in particular, processes on the interpersonal plane (Vygotsky, 1978) are more than merely an extension of those established in their prior experience in the home. They require a whole new information set to become internalised, not merely as what is expected by their particular nursery, but also what is passed on to them through the setting of wider social, cultural and historical forces that contribute to the construction and delivery of early schooling.

The role of the child in her own learning: a socio-cultural perspective

A socio-cultural approach to the learning of bilingual children helps our understanding because it emphasises the inter-relatedness of the social, cultural and linguistic aspects of children's learning. This perspective also supports our understanding of bilingual children's language and learning development within their new social environment with its different cultural rules and expectations. And it can take account of the individual child's social and cultural heritage and experience from the home. This view is consistent with Vygotsky's claim 'that in order to understand the individual, it is necessary to understand the social relations in which the individual exists' (Wertsch, 1991: 25-26). This view of the primary significance of social experience for children's development and learning has particular application for children entering an English medium, schooling setting in which they have yet to learn the language. Children learning a second or additional language are dispossessed of much of their home learning as well as use of their first language, in the unfamiliar context of the nursery setting. So the social processes and how these actually develop are of crucial importance. We saw in Chapter 2, for example, how Samia utilised the play opportunities at home as part of the process of internalising the social rules she was learning simultaneously in the nursery.

Bakhtin's theory of dialogism reinforces the idea that language is socio-culturally situated: in producing an utterance a speaker necessarily invokes a social language, 'and this social language shapes what the individual voice can say' (Wertsch, 1991: 59). What an individual says is unique but it is constructed from social languages and this process involves a type of dialogicality which Bakhtin called 'ventriloquation'.

> The word in language is half someone else's. It becomes 'one's own' only when the speaker populates it with his own intention, his own accent, when he appropriates the word, adapting it to his own semantic and expressive intention. Prior to this moment of appropriation....it exists in other people's mouths, in other people's concrete contexts, serving other people's intentions: it is from there that one must take the word, and make it one's own (Bakhtin, 1981: 293-294).

Bakhtin envisages a process whereby one voice speaks through another voice or voice type in a social language (Wertsch, 1991). This process is an aspect of language learning and language use which both transmits social and cultural meanings and enables individuals to convey personal meaning and intention relating to their specific context. Wertsch *et al* comment: 'From the perspective of how children come to be socialised such that they can function successfully in particular socio-cultural settings, then, the issue is one of learning how to ventriloquate through new social languages' (Wertsch *et al*, 1993: 345). Although Bakhtin had in mind speakers who share the same national or regional language, his view that language is specific to social context has important implications for children learning English as an additional language, since their task is not about learning a language in the abstract but about how to construct a 'voice' which accommodates the context of situation.

The child mediating her own learning

The constructs of scaffolding, guided participation, and the potential for synergy between child and a mediator help us to explore different perspectives on the ways in which 'more capable others' support learning.

Scaffolding

Central to a socio-cultural perspective is the notion of young children as novices or apprentices learning alongside more knowledgeable others. These mediators may be teacher, adult, sibling or peer, assisting children's participation in learning contexts within the frame of Vygotsky's ZPD. Wood, Bruner and Ross (1976) called the process by which an adult assists a child to carry out a task which would otherwise be beyond the child's capability 'scaffolding'. Bruner (1983) extended the 'scaffolding' metaphor by applying it to an analysis of interactions between mother and child to assist early language development. The central purpose of scaffolding was to enable the learner to focus upon manageable aspects of the task. The adult is able to control the demands of the task so that they are neither too simple or too complex. Wood (1998) offers an interesting explanation of the underlying reason for the necessity of scaffolding learning. Uncertainty is central to human ability, argues Wood, and in unfamiliar situations there is a high level of uncertainty so the ability to learn is reduced. Assisting the child by breaking down a complex task into manageable steps lessens their uncertainty and increases their learning potential.

> Children, being novices of life in general, are potentially confronted with more uncertainty than the more mature, and, hence, their abilities to select, remember and plan are limited in proportion. Without help in organising their attention and activity, children may be overwhelmed by uncertainty. (Wood, 1998: 165)

This may to varying degrees describe the experience of bilingual children entering nursery and it calls into question whether adequate scaffolding is provided to enable them to overcome their 'uncertainty'.

Guided participation

Rogoff (1990) uses the concept of 'guided participation'. She argues that whereas the zone of proximal development has been related to the context of schooling, the concept of guided participation can capture not only practices in different societies and cultures but also the involvement of children in routine activities in their communities outside education settings.

The perspective adopted by Rogoff is useful when considering the situation of children entering formal schooling from minority communities with belief systems and practices which may differ from those of the majority community or those assumed by the education system. First, it can take account of practices and experiences in the home which may help to highlight the adjustment bilingual children have to make when they enter school. Second, by identifying and comparing different community practices, those of the nursery setting become recognised as one set only. But it is these practices, and those of the education system as a whole which privilege literacy and academic learning, that have to be adopted by bilingual children for their future success. By acknowledging other cultural practices Rogoff helps to give value to developmental experience for children from minority cultural groups which takes place outside the classroom. Finally, her approach brings out the active participation of children.

Rogoff *et al* (1998) define 'guided participation' as follows:

Guided participation stresses tacit forms of communication in the verbal and non-verbal exchanges of daily life and the distal arrangements involved in the regulation of children's activities, material goods, and companions. The notion of guided participation emphasises the active role of children in both observing and participating in the organised societal activity of their caregivers and companions. In this more inclusive approach, the aim is to encompass more of the daily activities in which children participate and develop skill in and understanding of the valued approaches of their cultural community. (1998: 229)

Emphasising the active participation of children, Rogoff (1990) offers further helpful refinement to theories of development based on principles established by Vygotsky. Rather than viewing what children learn from social interaction as a matter of 'internalising' an external process on the interpersonal plane to the intrapersonal plane in a two-step process, Rogoff suggests that the process is, rather, 'appropriation'. Because they are already participants, children *appropriate* a changed understanding through their own involvement. The concept of appropriation, instead of internalisation, is useful when considering bilingual children who come to nursery with a well established set of understandings based on home experience and cultural practices. What they need to do in the nursery is to appropriate a new set of understandings through their participation in the practices that apply in the new setting.

Synergy, the role of the mediator and agency

For Rogoff, guided participation assists the child in appropriating changed understandings. But as Gregory (2001) points out, the term 'guided participation' implies 'an unequal relationship between participants in that learning is unidirectional from the older or more experienced person to the younger child' (2001: 303). Moreover the terminology used by Rogoff does not highlight the part played by the more proficient teacher, adult, sibling or peer in engaging the child in the ZPD. In her study of siblings playing and working together, Gregory suggests that the reciprocity involved stimulates the development of both children. She extends the ways in which scaffolding has generally been interpreted in her use of the notion of the 'synergy' which takes place between siblings. '...we refer to the interaction between the children as a synergy, a unique reciprocity whereby siblings act as adjuvants in each other's learning, i.e. older children 'teach' younger siblings and at the same time develop their own learning' (2001: 309). Indeed, she suggests that it is, in Vygotskian terms, a mediational means for transforming social engagement on an interpersonal plane into knowledge internalised on an intrapersonal plane. Drawing on Cole's (1985) understanding of the process of 'internalisation', she argues that 'synergy is the key mediator through which knowledge... is internalised' (Gregory, 2001: 311).

Using the notion of synergy emphasises Gregory's interest in how learning involves processes of coming together both within and between people. She views the process of blending different cultural, linguistic and literacy experiences as a form of syncretism which arises from the synergy produced by the child's engagement with mediators and which ultimately influences the shaping of identity. Describing the literacy experience of Bangaldeshi women, for instance, she comments:

> When Ros explains how her Bengali classes enriched her knowledge about literacy in the English school, she highlights the syncretism of different literacies and different ways of becoming literate in all the women's lives. Reading fairytales, comics and reading schemes in English opens new worlds which blend with and transform the traditional worlds of the Bengali and Qur'anic classes and vice versa. But literacy only symbolises a wider syncretism between languages and identities taking place in the women's lives. (Gregory and Williams, 2000: 140)

Gregory also points to the importance of understanding the role of the mediator (2000: 11) from a socio-cultural perspective. The mediator provides the means for 'scaffolding' learning (in Bruner's terms), or engages in 'guided participation' which enables appropriation of new understanding (in Rogoff's terms), or contributes to the synergy which assists the syncretism that leads to new knowledge (in Gregory's terms). For Gregory the mediator is not just the teacher but may equally be a sibling, a peer or another adult. The mediator assists the child not only to take on new learning but more particularly to take on a new culture and language alongside the existing one. The role of the mediator is likely to be highly influential in most contexts, but nowhere more so than in the case of a bilingual classroom assistant. For bilingual children entering the nursery the presence of such a mediator of language, culture and learning may be a crucial to how a child is enabled to 'appropriate' all that is expected in the new setting.

Taking the highly constrained situation of a bilingual child new to English entering the nursery as a starting point, the construct of agency is illuminated by the ways in which the children make their own choices and exercise some control.

As Pollard (2000: 127) states:

the child must make sense of new experiences, and in so doing will also contribute to the experiences of others. It is only when the socially created 'planned intervention' of curriculum and schooling is introduced that the child is repositioned as 'pupil' and becomes viewed, in terms of the education system as deficient. We may conclude that children have their own integrity and agency...

This has resonances for young bilingual children beginning school whose starting points may be viewed as deficit because unless their teachers have a language and cultural match, the learning that is taking place will be far less visible than for English speaking children.

The role of asserting possession in the Silent Period

We have seen that the need to engage in social interaction with peers is a particular difficulty for young developing bilingual children in the nursery. They face the 'double bind' (Tabors, 1997) of needing the language they do not yet know to be able to interact, yet also needing social interaction to be able to learn the language. Wong-Fillmore (1979) found that children differed markedly in their response to the problem of making contact with native speakers. She identified some broad social strategies children used and suggested that social confidence was important for successful language learning. Thompson's (1999) study of social networks similarly emphasised the importance of social interaction and suggested that same-language friendships assist enculturation of new arrivals in the nursery.

Second language acquisition studies have established recognisable early stages for second/additional language development and have drawn particular attention to the silent period. Research examining the early stages of development has not been widely acknowledged in the UK (NALDIC, 1998). Yet the value of recognising these stages is that they can be used to provide a framework against which practitioners can exercise their judgement about individual children's progress, and provide appropriate learning opportunities

When entering an unfamiliar early years setting many children go through a period observed by researchers, often described as the silent period. The 'non-verbal' period is a more accurate term, as children may still interact non-verbally.

During the silent or non-verbal period, children are taking time to acclimatise to their new environment and begin to tune in to the sounds of the setting and know what is expected. Children may begin to rehearse the language silently to themselves, and, in time, practise the utterances in 'private speech' until they have the confidence to try out the language for communicative purposes. They require reassurance and encouragement so they need to feel they are accepted members of the group.

Clarke (1992) suggests ten strategies to support children's language development during this stage:

1. Continued talking even when children do not respond
2. Persistent inclusion in small groups with other children
3. Use of varied questions
4. Inclusion of other children as the focus in the conversation
5. Use of the first language
6. Acceptance of non-verbal responses
7. Praising of minimal effort
8. Expectations to respond with repeated words and/or counting
9. Structuring of programme to encourage child to child interaction
10. Provide activities which reinforce language practice through role play.

(Clarke, 1992: 17-18)

Children then begin to use single words or formulaic phrases and repetition in the early stages of learning English. They use formulae and chunks of ready-made phrases in routine situations. This enables the learners to begin to interact with others. Clarke (1996) found that the quality of interaction between teacher and child was particularly important, while Saville-Troike (1988) concluded that 'reflective' rather than 'socially assertive' children are more likely to be successful second/additional language learners over time, though this does not seem to be reflected in this current study. While these and other studies have shed light on the early stages of learning English in the nursery setting, they have tended to focus on language acquisition in a given situation without identifying the wider constructed context of schooling or its relationship with the home and community context.

Summary: socio-cultural perspectives

Socio-cultural perspectives thus give us a theoretical framework for viewing Nazma, Samia and Maria's learning. These multiple perspectives are closely inter-related; indeed they are mutually implicit and interdependent. Agency was related to Vygotsky's socio-cultural view of learning which itself incorporates and depends on language use that is realised in social context.

Accounts of language offered by Bakhtin and the 'situated' nature of children's participation and the role of adults in supporting learning showed the importance of social context. The process of second/additional language learning is dependent on social and cultural setting. Each perspective had something to say about the way young bilingual children make their way in their first year of formal schooling.

In chapter 7 we return to each of the three areas discussed in this chapter and argue for a refined and extended theoretical framework in which to situate young children as they become bilingual in school.

5

The Inner Layer: the child

Invisible learning in the nursery

Samia has moved onto the carpet where children are playing with a Brio wooden train set.

She is silent whilst playing on her own. Another child joins in......

1 Samia: No, mine

                      Not yours [to another child]

                      No (indistinct) big boy

Samia: Look [to another boy]

[There is no response]

[Audio recording during the first term in nursery]

This chapter describes how Nazma, Samia and Maria respond as individuals to the nursery situation, find their own way through early schooling and make choices. How they do so reveals the particular strategy a child will discover and adopt in order to deal with a situation in which she finds herself. Each child responds to the flow of experience with all the resources at their disposal, displayed through their individual personal characteristics and personalities. Although certain children have common strategies to deal with situations which are very similar, each child tackles the task of learning to learn in nursery differently and each strategy is adapted individually. The strategies highlight the girls' ability to manage the situation and set about learning the language and culture of early schooling. When we follow this interpretation, we can see aspects of the children's learning which remain invisible to their teachers and which demonstrate their individuality and developing control over their learning.

INVISIBLE LEARNING

CHILD		AT NURSERY			AT HOME	
	Page	Transcript Title	Learning Strategy	Page	Transcript Title	Learning Strategy
Samia	61	No, mine!	Asserting possession	82	Nursery rhymes	Practising and rehearsing
	64	Bathroom	Practising and rehearsing	83	School story	Practising and rehearsing
	65	Knees and toes	Practising and rehearsing			
	67	Brick play	Asking questions			
	68	Caterpillar	Asking questions			
	69	Pussy cat	Language play			
	70	Colouring	Knowing colours			
	70	Percy	Conforming to adult expectations			
Maria	62	Cakes	Asserting possession	83	Spice Girls song	Practising and rehearsing
	63	Writing table	Asserting possession	84	When I'm a big girl	Conforming to adult expectations
	65	Shapes and colours	Practising and rehearsing			
	66	Repetition	Practising and rehearsing			
	71	Painting	Conforming to adult expectations			
	72	I drawed a fire engine	Taking risks			
	72	Mama I love you	Being centre of attention			
Nazma	73	Papoo	Practising and rehearsing	85	Twinkle twinkle	Practising and rehearsing
	75	Silence	Silence	86	Noreen	Practising and rehearsing
	76	Butterfly	Drawing on home experiences	87	1, 2, 3, 4, 5	Language play
				88	Kitchen	Asking questions
	77	Lemon, yuk!	Finding a cultural mediator	88	Good girls'	Conforming to adult expectations

Although the children spend long periods of time on their own, making minimal engagement within the setting and not speaking as they acclimatise to their new environment, they respond to their situations as key players and agents of their own learning.

Starting nursery as a bilingual learner is a difficult and crucial time for the children. This is highlighted in the spoken evidence collected in the data – in both English and mother tongue – which indicates their response to the early days in nursery and adds up to a revealing picture of their experience.

The role of asserting possession in the silent period
Asserting possession strategy
Some children may face a time in their new and unfamiliar social context when other children need to be taken into account, just when the demands of their insecurity enforce disengagement rather than engagement to protect personal space and possessions. Early examples of children's attempts to use English often stem from a social imperative to protect the self. This occurs before their early attempts to use the new language to respond to an adult or other children in their expanding social learning contexts. It plays into the 'double bind' (Tabors, 1997): the dependence of language acquisition on the acceptance of children with little English by their English speaking peers before social interaction can take place.

In the following transcript we can see how Samia's responses play into or promote this double bind. Her need to protect her play materials discourages interaction with another child and, at this stage, self protection is the priority. Once we recognise Samia's experience of the double bind, we can see her assertiveness as a stage in her progress towards social integration and an important strategy for getting by during her first few months in nursery.

SAMIA

'No, mine!' transcript during the first term

Samia has moved onto the carpet where children are playing with a Brio wooden train set.

She is silent whilst playing on her own.

1 Samia:	No, mine!
	Not yours [to another child]
	No (indistinct) big boy
Samia:	Look [to another boy]

61

[There is no response.

Talk is going on around her while she is playing, but it is not addressed to Samia].

5 Child 1:	No, this is mine
Samia:	It's mine
Child 1:	You're hurting me, get away from me.
Samia:	That's mine
Child1:	Hey, you're breaking mine

When Samia protests to a child playing near her who has taken a piece of her model by saying, 'no, mine, not yours,' the other child ignores it. Samia makes two further attempts and the interaction helps her to establish her presence – a necessary precursor to the more constructive interaction with other children which will become the principal stimulus for her language learning. Interestingly however, her social isolation still dominates in the nursery at this point. The other children playing near her talk to each other, but she is excluded as her English is not yet sufficient to enable her to initiate and hold interactions constructively, neither on her own terms nor on her peers'.

Later in the same nursery session, Samia uses the strategy of self-assertion again:

| Samia: | Shut up, I teacher |
| | Not yours here OK |

MARIA

During her early days at nursery, Maria actively listens to the English spoken by other children at play, and to the adults' interactions with her. In the three taped sessions during her first term at nursery, Maria is evidently more confident in her conversations with adults, particularly the BCA and nursery nurses. She plays alongside other children and participates in on-going nursery activities. During the first recording at nursery, Maria is sitting at the dough table with two English-speaking girls. They have an extended conversation about the cakes they are making with the playdough. Maria listens to their conversation but does not join in. But we note from the following transcript how she introduces the strategy of self-assertion, to protect her playdough.

Cakes transcript during the first term

| 1 | Child 1: | Look at my cake |

		Look at my cake
		There's a cherry on
		This cake has got a cherry on top
5		This is my cake
		My cake is so heavy I can't lift it up
	Child 2	It's a giant
	Child 1	Yes, it's a giant cake
		Oh, the cherry fell off
10		Look
		[to Maria]
		Oh you're making a pancake?
	Child 2	Where shall I put them?
	Child 1	Put them on a spoon
		Can I have some more cake?
15	Maria	No

This is the only recorded example of Maria speaking with other children in nursery during her first term. It is not until her third term that Maria shows greater confidence in her use of English. During one session at nursery, she employs a range of strategies for her interactions with other children.

Maria is at the writing table, writing her name. Another child joins her and Maria's self-assertion is particularly evident.

Writing table transcript during the third term

1	Maria	Let my do it
		Let my show you
	Child 1	No
		What you have to do?
5	Maria	Let my do it
		Get off
		You off that
		You come down, down, down

		[singing to herself, to the tune of Twinkle, twinkle]
	Child 1	[indistinct]
10	Maria	No, it's mine
	Child 1	Why you got that on? [referring to the radio mic.]
	Maria	I know

The role of the child in her own learning
Practising and rehearsing strategy

By the end of their first term in nursery, both Maria and Samia are more confident and are seen taking risks in their use of English. They deploy the strategies of practising and rehearsing English, asking questions and playing with language in the context of a play activity with their peers, or, in Samia's case, in the bathroom at nursery with her friend Bathriye. These are contexts in which the girls feel safe so are more comfortable in taking risks with their English language learning.

SAMIA

Bathroom transcript at the end of the first term

1	Samia:	Go back OK
		Go back
		Me no
		Go back
5		Go
	Bahriye:	Me no go
	Samia:	Go
		I have [indistinct]
	Bahriye:	[indistinct]
10	Samia:	Go
		Go back
	Bahriye:	Me toilet
	Samia:	Me
	Bahriye:	Ouch, shut the door or I will hit you

During small group time, the children sing the song 'Heads shoulders knees and toes' while they drink their milk. Samia joins in the 'knees and toes' chorus. Then it is time to go and play in the garden.

'Knees and toes' transcript at the end of the first term

1 Teacher:	Samia can you finish your milk
Samia:	knees and toes, knees and toes
	Knees and toes
	Knees and toes
5	Knees and toes
	Knees and toes
	Knees and toes
	Knees and toes
	Knees and toes
10	Knees and toes
	Knees and toes
	Knees and toes

[Samia is singing to herself]

Teacher:	Are you still singing Samia?
	Sing it with me
15 Samia:	Heads shoulders knees toes
Teacher:	The word in the middle is 'and'

Samia's language practice derives from the more significant classroom routines and activities such as songs, which are initiated through adult-led contexts. This practice is also seen operating at home.

During her third term at nursery, we witness examples of Maria practising her English both on her own and with adults. In the following excerpt, she also demonstrates her knowledge of key words, for example shapes and colours.

MARIA

Shapes and colours transcript at the end of the third term

[Maria is at a cutting activity with a nursery nurse – NN]

1	NN	What are you going to do now Maria, some cutting?

	Maria	Round and round and cut and cut [speaking to herself]
		Cut and cut and cut and cut
	NN	Are you cutting a ball?
5		What shape is it?
		What shape is it?
	Maria	Triangle
	NN	Triangle yes very good
		Shall I get you some crayons to colour it with in a minute?
10		What colour crayons would you like?
Maria		Red
NN		Red, any other colours?
Maria		Blue
NN		Red and blue OK

In lines 2 and 3 Maria is practising her English, speaking to herself in line 2 and out loud in line 3. This is an important part of her English language development and the cutting activity gives her a good opportunity and focus to practise these language forms and display key vocabulary. We see that Maria can show her knowledge of key vocabulary items for successful learning in the nursery, in this case colours and shapes. The conversation shows us that she understands and can respond appropriately to the adult's questioning routine. The nursery nurse supports Maria's English.

During her interactions with adults, Maria uses repetition as a key strategy for engaging in learning activities. Her repetition thus serves to emphasise her communication and intent. In the following transcript during the first recording in nursery, Maria responds to the nursery nurse by repeating her last utterance.

Repetition transcript during the first term

[Maria is making a face using paper shapes]

1	NN	Right what's that?
		What is it?
		It's an eye, isn't it
	Maria	Eye

5	NN	Good girl
		How many have you got?
		One
	Maria	One
	NN	Two
10	Maria	Two
	NN	Right, what colour are your eyes?

This transcript is an excerpt from a longer interaction with the nursery nurse, during which Maria uses repetition as a way of engaging with the adult and practising her English. She is rewarded with warm praise (see for example, line 5) and she clearly enjoys the sustained one-to-one interaction with the nursery nurse.

SAMIA
Asking questions strategy

During her first term at nursery, Samia plays with bricks in the small construction area on the carpet. The BCA joins her during her solitary play and the conversation with Samia is in Pahari – so shown in italics.

Brick play transcript during the first term

1 Samia:	*What is this, Teacher?*
	Where shall I put this?
BCA:	*What is this?*
Samia:	*This is a duck*
5 BCA:	*What colour is the duck?*
Samia:	*This is a blue colour and this is a red colour*
	I couldn't find the same piece
BCA:	*Is this the piece?*
Samia:	*No this doesn't fit here*
10 BCA:	*Try it*
	Does it fit?
Samia:	*No, it doesn't*

We can see that Samia's language use in Pahari matches the expectations for a native English speaker of the same age. Samia asks questions to engage the BCA in her learning (lines 1 and 2) and uses key words to display her knowledge. It is clear that working with a BCA and using her mother tongue enables Samia to engage actively with learning in nursery.

By the end of her two terms at nursery, Samia has developed confidence in her use of English. She takes risks during her conversations with children while playing.

During a session at nursery, Samia is doing an alphabet caterpillar puzzle with Bahriye. She is beginning to move on from a stage when formulaic language predominates. She recognises different forms of language but has not yet sorted out pronoun substitution possibilities. She has an extended conversation with her friend in English (45 lines) and uses the strategies of asking questions, and practising English. This enables her to actively generate her own learning.

Caterpillar puzzle transcript during the second term

1 Samia:	We saw it caterpillar in'it?
Bahriye:	Yeah, like this fat H caterpillar
Samia:	Yeah that caterpillar [laughing]
	It was there I think
	Go there
	Go there
	Where that go?
Bahriye:	Where that go?
	Go there
10 Samia:	Where?
	No that don't go there
Bahriye:	Here
Samia:	Where that go?
	Silly fat sausage
15	Where that go?
	That go there
	Where that go?
	That goes in here

The repeated use of the question 'where that go?' helps Samia to direct the activity of doing the caterpillar puzzle and at the same time practise her English in a natural and stress free context. Her Pahari speaking friend, Bahriye, joins in with the repetition and asking questions and provides a supportive framework for the whole activity. The use of the colloquial phrase 'silly fat sausage' demonstrates her developing knowledge of English, obviously drawn from peer social interaction. She is clearly confident in taking risks with her language use, for example the question tag *in'it*, yet another colloquialism.

Language play strategy
Having fun with language is an important strategy for Samia during her second – and last – term at nursery. She is no longer using simple self-assertion but genuine language play on a mutual level with native English speaking peers. We see her in the nursery bathroom, taking a lead and imitating her friend in language play with the words 'pooh' and 'pussy'.

'Pussy cat' transcript during the second term

1 Samia:	Look teacher coming garden
	Pussy cat
Child A:	Dried a pooh
Samia:	Dried a pooh [laughs]
5 Child A:	Dried a pooh pooh
Samia:	Dried a pussy pussy
	Have it pussy
	Have your breakfast pussy

Samia is showing confidence and enjoyment in the interaction with her friend. Playing with language is a key strategy for getting by and learning in English. It is crucial for the development of spoken language and for the early literacy work she will encounter when she starts school the following term.

Samia and Maria have contrasting approaches to adults' expectations, both at home and in nursery. Recognising the special significance of responding appropriately to adults, Samia makes use of her developing English with some hesitancy, illustrating her need to control by minimising risk-taking. We can see how her strategies at nursery include 'responding without taking risks when addressed by adults', 'conforming to adult expectations' and 'joining in whenever possible'. A particularly significant strategy – both in nursery and in her school game at home with her brother – is using her knowledge of colours.

Knowing colours strategy
Percy transcript during the first term

1 Teacher:	We need different colours to do Percy
	What colour did we need to do his boots?
Samia:	Black
Teacher:	So we need some black to do his boots
5	What colour do we need to do his shirt?
Child A:	Green
Teacher:	What shall we use, dark green or light green?
	Most children want this one
	What about his waistcoat?
10 Child B:	Brown
Teacher:	Is that brown?
	Is that brown?
	Is that brown?

Samia and Maria alike have learnt the need to show their understanding of colours, as well as other key vocabulary items such as numbers and shapes through appropriate language use and interaction with adults.

Conforming to adult expectations strategy

When Samia is with adults she conforms to what she understands to be required of her. She does this well, picking up what is expected, thus reading and reacting well to the nursery environment. This is again evident when she is at nursery during a teacher-led small group activity. The children are asked to recall what they have done at nursery and this activity has a predictable routine which is repeated each day.

Colouring transcript during the first term

1 Teacher:	Shall we ask Samia what she did today?
	What did you do today? You tell us...
	What did you do? [whispered]

Samia:	[indistinct]
5 Teacher:	Did you play with some shapes that were different colours?
Samia:	Colouring
Teacher:	Colouring – you did some colouring
	Perhaps you did that after the puzzles
	What colours did you put on your picture?

[BCA interprets the question in Pahari. Samia says *I can't remember*]

Samia knows how to conform to adult expectation – to answer a question directed to her only when she knows the appropriate word. Colouring, as we saw, is a key word for Samia and she uses it appropriately to answer the teacher's question, without risk of further elaboration and her consequent exposure and possible failure amongst her peers.

MARIA
Painting transcript during the first term

During the first recording in the nursery, Maria listens and responds appropriately to adults.

[Maria is in her small group, planning with the nursery nurse – NN]

1	NN	What would you like to do?
		Maria, what would you like to do?
		Maria
		Maria, what would you like to do?
5	Maria	Painting
	NN	Painting?
		Find your apron then
		Apron

Maria understands what is expected of her in the context of small group planning. She uses the appropriate word, 'painting', and then proceeds with the activity she has chosen.

Taking risks strategy
Maria is obviously confident in her conversations with adults at nursery, even during the first few months of early schooling, as we see in a book-sharing session with a nursery nurse.

'I drawed a fire engine' transcript during the first term

[Maria is sharing a book *Starting School* with a nursery nurse. She is talking about the pictures]

1	Maria	Mummies and daddies
		Sisters
		Coats
		Toilets
5		Do you know something, I drawed a fire engine
	NN	Did you, lovely
		Put it in your book bag

In the context of the book corner and sharing a book with a familiar adult, Maria is confident enough to name familiar items in English (lines 1-4). However, her contribution in line 5 is her longest utterance recorded in nursery during her first term, and shows her willingness to take risks with her developing English language.

Being centre of attention strategy

As the transcripts show, Maria is becoming confident and motivated in the company of adults in the nursery. She clearly enjoys the opportunity to be the centre of attention, particularly with one of the nursery nurses. This is echoed in her experience at home, where she is able to take a leading role with adults and manipulate the family.

We see her in the music room with a nursery nurse.

'Mama I love you' transcript during the third term

1	NN	What shall we do then shall we sing some songs?
	Maria	Mama
	NN	Hey?
	Maria	Mama I love you
5	NN	Mama I love you – do you know that song?
		Who sings that?
		Spice Girls
		Sing it for me then

	Maria	Mama I love you I don't care you my friend
10	NN	Oh that's lovely my little girl likes that song
		What else can you sing?
	Maria	Ba ba black sheep
	NN	Go on then
	Maria	Ba ba black sheep have you any wool yes sir yes sir three bags full

Maria is clearly enjoying this opportunity to demonstrate her repertoire of English songs . This is a role to which she has become accustomed and, by the end of her first year of early schooling, she has been able to manipulate situations that let her show what she can do well.

Practising and rehearsing strategy
NAZMA

In contrast, the record of Nazma's first term at nursery creates an unhappy picture. Nazma is clearly distressed by the difficulties of early transition from home to school and this is most evident from her frequent crying, sucking fingers, holding her sister Yasmin's or Mussarat's hand or clinging to her mother. Mussarat plays an important role during this transition period. For Nazma, it is likely that this early experience of schooling will form the basis for all her future learning.

In analysing the strategies Nazma uses at school, we see her inside her shell. She clings to the powerful strategy of silence when she is with nursery staff and other children.

There are no recordings when Nazma speaks in English during her first term, nor of her playing with or talking to other children in the nursery, other than in their mother tongue with her sister Yasmin.

Papoo transcript during the fourth term

It took until her fourth term before Nazma learned to participate in nursery activities and began to do what was expected of her. But there is little evidence of her interacting with other children. An exception is the transcript of Nazma speaking with her sister Yasmin. By then Yasmin had moved into the Reception class in an adjoining classroom. The nursery and reception classes share the same toilets and bathrooms and Yasmin and Nazma meet in the toilets by chance.

1	Nazma:	*Papoo* [calling out Yasmin's nickname]
		There's wee there
		You can eat this
		It's pizza you eat it [N has a piece of plastic pizza in her hand]
5	Yasmin:	*No*
	Nazma:	*Go on eat it it's hot*
		It's pizza – go on
	Yasmin:	*I'll tell*
	Nazma:	*We've been to the toilet* [talking to another child]
10		*Dirty*
		Very very tightly
		Wash it up do this [N is singing this]
		Don't touch it [referring to the microphone]
		Teacher will hit you
15		Wash up [N resumes her singing]

Here Nazma is behaving like a typical four-year old. She has a piece of plastic pizza in her pocket taken from the home corner, and she is lively in her playful exchange with her elder sister. She is quite animated and demonstrates her ability to engage in imaginative play in Pahari (lines 3-7). In the safe context of the bathroom, Nazma tries to engage her sister in play. Note that Yasmin, now in Reception, does not allow this play to develop and ends the interaction with her threat to inform the nursery staff: 'I'll tell'.

Nazma uses the context to practise a song from nursery 'wash it up, do this'. She is confident in this context to vocalise and practise her English with her sister. This occasion, however, was the only example of such an interaction. Nazma is socially isolated in nursery and relishes the chance appearance of her sister Yasmin in the bathroom providing a lifeline for Nazma's social expression at this stage.

Silence strategy

Over the four terms in nursery, we have no examples of data recording interaction between Nazma and the nursery teachers or nursery nurses. This is surprising considering how long she has been there. Her learning of English depends vitally on interaction with adults and children at school but she never engages with the English-speaking staff in nursery, so can find no way of knowing what adults expect. Consequently joining in whenever possible or indeed responding without taking risks when addressed by an adult are not options for her, whereas for Samia and Maria these are successful strategies.

Nazma adopts an alternative strategy: be unobtrusive and be silent for the great majority of her time in nursery. An exception to this arose within the context created by the presence of the BCA, Mussarat, who was significant in the recordings made in nursery. It appears that Pahari is the principal source of cognitive and linguistic development for Nazma. The use of her mother tongue is virtually her only lifeline to learning. Without Pahari, and the presence of Mussarat or her sister, she appears wholly isolated, in effect, trying to function in the context of a foreign language.

In this example of the nursery teacher trying to engage Nazma during her first term by sharing books with her in the book corner, Nazma is silent throughout.

Silence transcript during the first term

1	Miranda:	Do you want this one? [to Nazma]
		Thomas and the dinosaur
		The engine's big
		Do you want that one?
5		The very hungry caterpillar
		In the light of the moon a little egg lay on the leaf
		One Sunday morning the warm sun came up
		And pop out of the egg came a tiny and very hungry caterpillar
		Pigs
10		Hens
		Sheep
		Finished?
		Read it to Nazma [to another child]

Nazma's strategy of silence demonstrates her resolve to take control over her learning. Her response to the demands of nursery and the expectations of adults is to present a wall of silence.

Drawing on home experiences strategy

There are other times when Nazma responds to the BCA in mother tongue and makes a contribution based on home experiences. Through Mussarat, a mediator of language and culture, Nazma can draw on her home experiences and engage with and find meaning in the learning experiences at school.

Butterfly transcript during the first term

The children are working in a small group with Mussarat.

Mussarat tells the story of *The Very Hungry Caterpillar* in Pahari.

1   Nazma: *We eat it at home* [pointing to picture of watermelon in book]

                  We eat it [excitedly]

[Nazma joins in with Mussarat, sharing the counting of fruit in the book in English]

       Mussarat: He was a beautiful butterfly

       Nazma: *I've seen a butterfly in my garden*

5   Mussarat: *How many eyes?*

       Nazma: *Two eyes*

                  One came in my garden and I hit it

This excerpt is a rare vignette of Nazma at her most responsive. This is the only time we see her being able to contribute her personal experience to the storytelling session with the BCA. Nazma's spontaneous response to the picture of the butterfly at the end of the book is to relate it to her personal experience of butterflies in her garden. Mussarat can then build on her contribution by asking how many eyes it had. But, retaining interest in her wish to express, Nazma continues with her own story using her first language fluently. Here we see her confidence as she is able to contribute within a small group, using the developing skills of her own language appropriately. It contrasts dramatically with her silence and her unwillingness to engage during most of the nursery recordings.

Finding a cultural mediator strategy

The crucial importance of Mussarat as the mediator of culture and language for Nazma during her early days of schooling is highlighted in the next transcript. Nazma found the transition from home more difficult than Samia and Maria and she spoke only when Mussarat was present.

We are given clear insights into the role of Nazma's mother tongue. For Nazma Pahari had been the basis for the greater part of her cognitive and linguistic development to date. There was little opportunity for assistance with her acquisition of English by peers for whom English was their mother tongue (Hirshler, 1994).

Without Pahari, and the opportunity to use it with a mediator, Nazma would be entirely isolated in a context where only English is spoken. Her mother tongue represents an ongoing bond between home and school, and thus an important continuity between the two domains. The tension for Nazma is to make the adjustment from home to school without losing the language and culture that sustain her.

Nazma's ability to engage with Mussarat and to use her mother tongue for learning is again evident here.

'Lemon, yuk!' transcript during the first term

1	Mussarat:	*What's this?*
	Nazma:	*Apples*
	Mussarat:	*What's this?*
	Nazma:	*Pears*
5	Mussarat:	*What's this?*
	Nazma:	*Lemon, yuk! I don't like that* [making a face]
	Mussarat:	*Don't you like it because it's sour?*
	Nazma:	*Yes*
	Mussarat	*1,2,3 green apples*
10	and Nazma:	[counting together]
	Mussarat	*1,2,3,4 pears* [counting together]
	and Nazma:	
	Nazma:	*We eat them, we like them,*
		We get them, we go to a shop and we buy apples and pears...
15		*We went to the shops with mum and Hasnan*
		And we bought lollies
		We had Hasnan's birthday
		We went in a big mosque and there were lots of people [the 'mosque' was in fact a hall]
20		*Friends and everybody was there.*
		There was cake
		I went with Hasnan to the shops. (Drury, 1997)

This conversation is embedded in Nazma's experience of family and culture and illustrates the importance for her of building on home experiences. Firstly, the opportunity to sit and look at a book with Mussarat gives her an appropriate context to relate a story from her home experience at some length. She talks about significant events in her life, knowing that Mussarat will understand. Secondly, Nazma knows that Mussarat will be able to interpret the meaning of her stories. Nazma knows the names of different fruits in her mother tongue and speaks clearly and fluently about them and about her family life. The crucial role of bilingual staff is highlighted here, as this is the only occasion when Nazma can communicate and begin to make sense of the strange world she has entered. Mussarat, as mediator, enables her to bridge the contexts of home and school and assists her to engage within the ZPD.

Summary: finding their way through nursery

This chapter has highlighted some of the ways in which Nazma, Samia and Maria find their way through nursery. Except for the part-time support of a bilingual classroom assistant, the language used by adults and most children in the nursery is English. It follows for early stage bilingual learners that they can have only limited communication with adults and their English speaking peers. Similarly, the expectations, values, manners and styles of interaction in the nursery are expressed through the culture of an English approach to early years education, schooling and the wider society. We begin to appreciate how adults in the nursery often know little about the real home experience of bilingual children, with the exception of the BCA. Thus it is left to the bilingual learners themselves to devise their own strategies to adapt to the language and culture of the nursery.

It becomes evident that although adults in the nursery have devised and employed a variety of ways to assist Nazma, Maria and Samia, the key player in the learning process is the child herself. As we come to see the girls taking control of their learning, we can recognise their responses as strategic. This perspective enables the analysis of data in terms of the strategies they employ throughout the different circumstances in which they find themselves.

For the children, the experience of being in school in an English medium environment with many children, and in a context which is formalised by rules, routines and expectations, is hugely important. Whilst adults might view the significance of this more in relation to education and life chances, for these bilingual children it is primarily about entering the unknown; about managing to get by in an unfamiliar, even alien, setting amongst unknown peers, new adult authority figures, and as part of new social and cultural values. These are strategies related not only to learning a new language but also to ways of coping within a new environment.

So we see that while they engage with the various aspects of nursery experience which involve a combination of language learning and language use for different purposes, and while others may influence the changing situation they face, it is Nazma, Samia and Maria who themselves take control of their learning.

Nazma is the one who is least able to relate to the new linguistic and cultural demands of nursery and appears to fear failure. She relies on the strategy of silence and being unobtrusive virtually throughout her four terms at nursery – and indeed, throughout Reception and Year 1. She does not talk to adults in nursery and any learning she does appears to depend totally on drawing on and sharing her home experiences with the BCA. Furthermore, she views herself as unable to do things at school and this turns out to be reflected in her end of Key Stage One SATs results.

Despite this, however, Nazma was not disempowered by her experience in nursery. The strategy she adopted with adults, to be silent, demonstrated her ability to manage the situation she encountered as she entered school. And she used her mother tongue strategically, through a linguistic and cultural mediator, as a means of finding her way through nursery.

The next chapter shows how these three children respond to their ongoing experience of early schooling when they are at home.

6

The Inner Layer: the child
Invisible learning at home

1	Nazma:	*What shall I do?*
	Hasnan:	12345 caught a fish alive
		Why did let it go
		Why it bit my finger
5	Nazma:	12345
		12345 fee for for
	Hasnan:	Caught a fish alive
		Not fort a fish alive
		12345
10		Not port a fish alive
		Caught a fish alive
	Nazma:	[singing to herself]
		12345
	Hasnan:	Not caught a forki tor
15	Yasmin:	12345 once I caught a fish alive

[Audio recording of Nazma playing with her siblings, Hasnan and Yasmin at home during her final term at nursery]

The inner layer of analysis in this chapter reveals how Nazma, Samia and Maria respond to their ongoing experience at home and how they continue to exercise considerable control with both the children and adults in the household. In all the transcripts we continue to show Pahari in italics and English in Roman script.

Practising and rehearsing strategy

SAMIA

During the first taping session in her home Samia has a conversation with her mother, grandmother and little brother Sadaqat.

Nursery rhymes transcript during the first term

1 Samia:	Ba ba black sheep
	Yes sir yes
	One two
	Twinkle twinkle
5	Ba ba
	Twinkle twinkle
	Twinkle twinkle
	I got pencils [to Grandmother]
	Twinkle twinkle
10 Grandmother:	*don't touch that*
Samia:	*I'm not going to talk*
	Mum, Sadaqat's got a sweet
	Head shoulders knees and toes [Sadaqat imitates her]
	No, head shoulders knees and toes
15	Eyes and nose and nose and eyes and mouth
	Touch your forehead, touch your hair, shoulder
	Knees and toes

Here Samia is singing, practising her English through the familiar nursery songs. She again involves her brother Sadaqat in her play. There are echoes of her teacher when she corrects his version of 'Heads shoulders knees and toes' (line 14). She skilfully code-switches from her nursery songs in English, to Pahari when she speaks to her grandmother or gives her brother important instructions.

Samia demonstrates increasing control when using her home language in the nursery with a bilingual adult and also with her mother and grandmother at home.

School story transcript during the second term

1	Mother:	*Have you been outside?*
	Samia:	*They both went outside with us*
		They sit with us
		They sat with us
5		*Then their mothers came*
		Their mothers went somewhere
		Then they came and they sat with us
		Then their mothers sat with us
		Then their mothers went to the Infant school
10		*Then they went home*

MARIA

Maria is at her most confident in her interactions with adults, both at home and in nursery. She takes every opportunity to manipulate the situation, particularly at home with her extended family of many adults, and takes charge of the conversations. At home, Maria is now the focus of attention in the family.

She is in control of the situation and displays a mature use of both Pahari and English in her interactions with adults at home. She uses English with her aunt and uncle and displays great skill in her code-switching with different members of her family.

Her mother tongue is advanced for her age and she uses complex language structures in her conversations with her father, mother and younger brother. In addition, she is strategic in the ways in which she conforms to adult expectations and offers monologues to the microphone (as below, for example), as this is her means of being centre of attention in the household.

Spice Girls song transcript during the third term

1	Uncle	*Come on speak English*
	Maria	You are

		I don't care
		I don't care
5		I don't care
		I don't care
	Aunt	That's a Spice Girls songs, isn't it?
		I don't care, I don't care
		How does it go?
10	Maria	Every song and then it's Spice Girl
		like that I don't care
	Aunt	Yeah that's a Spice Girls song
		Have you heard it
		It was on the TV
15	Maria	Sing it then
	Uncle	You sing it
	Maria	No you sing it
	Uncle	You don't want to sing, do you

Strategy of conforming to adults' expectations

In all the recordings at home, we see Maria conforming to the expectations of adults. The monologue in the first recording exemplifies their perceived expectations of the research study.

'When I'm a big girl' transcript during the first term

1	Maria	*When I am a big girl I'll be a doctor and drive a big car*
		My father's gone to Pakistan
		He said I'm going all by myself this time
		But when it's holiday time I'll take you
5		*We'll go together again*
		My father's in Pakistan
		One of my uncles is in Pakistan as well
		Iftikhar is in Pakistan – they are all there
		At school we've got playdough, *we do* cutting
10		*We do everything*
		We read books and we put books in the bag

Reflecting on this monologue, Mussarat commented, 'Maria's language and behaviour are mature for her age. She has a wide experience – this should help her to find her way in life and mix better in the classroom. She is ready to get on.' Maria can certainly now conform to adult expectations but, additionally, she is often able to dominate the family situation and take control. The ways in which the family involve her in their talk are supportive of her developing confidence as she experiences early schooling.

This strategic role is one she can act out during her early experiences of schooling and is also a role in which she is viewed as successful by adults at nursery.

Practising and rehearsing strategy
NAZMA
Nazma's home play with her siblings, particularly her sister Yasmin, gives us insights into the way she is learning which we do not see at school. Except for Mussarat, the nursery staff have an understanding of Nazma based largely on the way she presents in the nursery setting. Their view contrasts with her social interaction in the home. The recordings of Nazma at home are characterised by a focus on preparing and eating food – the tape recordings took place during lunchtime or after school and while playing with her siblings.

Here is Nazma playing with her elder sister Noreen. Noreen is encouraging her to practise her school English.

'Twinkle, twinkle' transcript during first term

1	Nazma:	[singing]
		Twinkle twinkle little star
		How I wonder what you are
		How I wonder what you are
5		Twinkle twinkle little star
		How I wonder what you are
		How I wonder what you are
	Noreen:	Good girl Nazma
		[Nazma is crying and goes upstairs]
10	Noreen:	Daddy's sleeping
	Nazma:	*Don't come inside*

	Hello hello
Noreen:	*Do you know* ba ba black sheep
Nazma:	Yes sir yes sir twinkle twinkle [laughing]

Nazma is performing to her sister's expectations, displaying her repertoire of English nursery rhymes. She is also code-switching between English and Pahari with ease. She is encouraged by Noreen with 'good girl Nazma' in teacher-like English. Noreen switches into Pahari to give a real instruction to her little sister; 'do you know ba ba black sheep'.

During her fourth term at nursery, Nazma practises her English with her sister at home after school, while playing outside in the yard.

Noreen Transcript during the fourth term

1	Nazma:	Little... [singing to herself]
		I went in the bed in the bed [singing]
		Why did you come there?
		Why did you come there?
		You can't by by there
	Noreen:	Can you ride this bike?
	Nazma:	Why did you do never playing do
		Why are you playing me you
	Noreen:	I said can you ride it?
	Nazma:	I got play with it
		[N. singing to herself]
	Nazma:	No you can't use
		You can't that
	Noreen:	Go inside
	Nazma:	Inside stay?
	Noreen:	I said you
	Nazma:	Shut up

In the context of her own back yard with her older sister, Nazma becomes free to practise her English. As she does not use this strategy in school, the opportunity to practise her limited English with her sister at home becomes crucial for her learning. However, on this occasion, Noreen is not willing to help Nazma with her English practice and persists with her questioning, 'can you ride this bike?' until finally she instructs Nazma to 'go inside'. Nazma's use of English in this comfortable and informal context shows us the fragility of her linguistic ability and confidence; a significant factor, perhaps, in her reluctance to respond within the more formal setting of the nursery.

Language play strategy

There are few examples of Nazma having fun with English, but again it is only during her play with siblings at home that the opportunity arises for language play. In one case, Nazma is playing with her elder brother Hasnan and her sister Yasmin and they are trying hard to make her speak English. Hasnan is teaching her a nursery song.

1 ,2, 3, 4 ,5 transcript during the fourth term

1	Nazma:	*What shall I do?*
	Hasnan:	12345 caught a fish alive
		Why did let it go
		Why it bit my finger
5	Nazma:	12345
		12345 fee for for
	Hasnan:	Caught a fish alive
		Not fort a fish alive
		12345
10		Not port a fish alive
		Caught a fish alive
	Nazma:	[singing to herself]
		12345
	Hasnan:	Not caught a forki tor
15	Yasmin:	12345 once I caught a fish alive

The older siblings clearly understand the importance of knowing the school nursery songs and Hasnan is using his own strategies (lines 8 – 11 and line 14) to teach her the words of the song '12345 Once I caught a fish alive'. As the strategies appear not to be working – Nazma simply repeats '12345' (line 13), Yasmin models the first line again for her (line 15). But Nazma still refuses to join in with their language play. As the youngest sibling, she is quite used to being the subject of her brothers' and sisters' 'teaching' and her role as the little sister includes occasionally being made fun of.

Unlike at nursery, Nazma plays a full part in her family life. The interactions at home with her mother and grandmother, the two key adults at home during the recordings, frequently focus on food and eating in the family and take place in Pahari. In this context Nazma is lively and confident.

Asking questions strategy
Kitchen transcript during the first term

[Yasmin and Nazma are in the kitchen with their mother]

1	Nazma:	*What are we going to do?*
	Mother:	*We need to eat then we need to get ready for nursery*
		What do you want?
	Nazma:	*Nothing*
5		*Mummy, look at this [referring to the microphone]*
		Mummy, what are you doing?
		Mummy?
	Mother:	*I'm going to cook chappattis for you*
	Yasmin:	*It's for Grandma and Nazma*
	Nazma:	*Why have they left this here?* [referring to the recording equipment]

This excerpt shows the two younger sisters going about normal family life with their mother. Nazma can ask questions in Pahari and engage fully while her mother is preparing lunch. Her questions show attention to and interest in the recording equipment and the microphone, still a novelty, as this was one of the earliest recordings.

Later on we see Nazma behaving appropriately during the mealtime and conforming to the adults' expectations.

Conforming to adults expectations strategy
'Good girls' transcript during the first term

[lunchtime with Grandmother, Yasmin and Nazma; Mother is cooking]

1	Mother:	*Now you sit here and be good sisters*

Yasmin: *Nazma is copying me*

This is mine

Mother: *Say thank you*

5   Y. and N.: Thank you mummy

Mother: Good girls

Nazma: *I can drink this*

Mother: *Eat quietly and don't fuss*

Grandmother: *Here you are*

10   Y. and N.: Thank you mummy

Nazma: Thank you thank you

Humpty dumpty [chanting to herself]

Y. and N. Twinkle twinkle little star

How I wonder what you are up a..

15   Twinkle twinkle little star

Jingle bells jingle bells

Nazma: *That's mine*

Give it to me [while eating]

Mother: *Have you finished*

20   *Shall we get ready*

Y. and N.: *Yes*

No

Mother: *Go and wash your hands*

Yasmin and Nazma show that they are able to conform to what their grand-mother and mother expect during lunchtime. Note that their mother encourages them to use English to say thank you (lines 4-6), the only time this occurred during the recordings at home. Again, the girls are practising their nursery songs. Nazma has taken the lead (line 12) and Yasmin joins in with her practice. By encouraging appropriate behaviour, their grandmother plays an important role, which the children respect.

Away from the larger family group, the two youngest children can use this familiar mealtime context to rehearse and practise in English on their own, in an almost abstract fashion, repeating the simple lines of a nursery rhyme or song.

Nazma uses a range of strategies with siblings and significant adults in the home context. She is responsive and quite lively. Her use of her mother tongue is confident and at a level normally expected for her age. The significance of learning English is underlined in her practising, rehearsing and playing with language while playing with her siblings. They, in turn, act as mediators of language and culture, helping Nazma to begin to bridge the transition between home and school.

Summary: invisible learning at home

Much of the developmental process which Nazma, Samia and Maria go through at home is not visible to the nursery teacher. The perception by her nursery teacher that 'Samia didn't speak much today', for example, is only a blinkered part of the reality of Samia's experience. Her rehearsal and practising of language rarely takes place in a context where she is observable by the teacher. The skills of Samia in play with her brother – her use of English, her facility with code-switching, her ability to engage and sustain her younger brother's involvement and her manipulation of school knowledge – are invisible to the nursery teacher. Similarly, Maria's successful rehearsal and practice of English rarely takes place with adults at nursery. The leading role she takes with her extended family at home is invisible to the nursery teacher, although sometimes she demonstrated her ability to be the centre of attention when interacting with a nursery nurse.

Nazma has no interactions with children in nursery except her sister Yasmin. This lack of social and linguistic interaction with her peers is likely to have had a detrimental effect on Nazma's learning and achievements during her early years of schooling. But we have witnessed some of her playful practising of English in the nursery bathroom. And her active engagement with her siblings at home, where she often participates in lively exchanges centred on family events, demonstrates her ability to practise and play with her newly acquired English. There are examples of the significant mediating role her siblings play, in their attempts to teach her English, particularly English nursery rhymes and songs.

As Samia and Maria go through the process of learning English while experiencing formal schooling for the first time, we saw, firstly, the control they command over their learning and the strategies they adopt to do so and, secondly, how much of this is invisible to the teacher. The detailed picture that is emerging enables us to recognise how the children themselves are at the centre of their learning.

In contrast to Samia and Maria, Nazma's response to early schooling has been to withdraw into a shell of silence in the nursery classroom. This can be viewed as also strategic, much like her persistent use of mother tongue with Mussarat in an English medium environment. Again these characteristics highlight the invisible aspects of bilingual children's experiences as they begin school.

Chapter 7 considers the implications of the research for educators of young bilingual children.

7

Implications for the education of young bilingual children

Samia has settled quietly into Nursery. She uses the planning board to find activities and mostly works alone at painting, jigsaws or sometimes in the imaginative area or construction area.

Samia didn't speak today – sometimes says one or two words. I gave her some ideas at Recall eg painting and she nodded agreement. [Interview with Samia's nursery teacher during her first term at nursery]

Consider the comment 'Samia didn't speak today' in the light of Samia's school game with her little brother at home. What can we learn from the learning experiences of Nazma, Samia and Maria that are invisible to their English-speaking teachers?

The stories of Samia, Maria and Nazma as they proceed through their first year's education signal the urgent need for action. They reveal the important knowledge about these young bilingual children's learning in their early schooling that went unrecognised by their nursery educators. The effects of this are hard to measure but the children's educational progress has almost certainly been held back as a result. Had the measures suggested at the end of this chapter been in place, they would have learned faster and probably been happier in nursery.

In their study of four children's learning, Pollard and Filer focused on the ways in which 'they learn and make their way through a succession of new situations and experiences ...' in contexts which 'contain challenges and threats which young children have to negotiate' (Pollard with Filer, 1996: 3). This book's exploration of three bilingual girls' ways of setting about learning in the early years of schooling shows the additional hurdles created by language.

We see that the various strategies the children employ for coping within the nursery context fit with Bruner's view of learning in action, 'in which the child is a protagonist – and agent, a victim, an accomplice' (Bruner, 1990:85).

The nursery context each girl entered was highly constrained, a structure of educational prerequisites determined by early years policy and practice. The context for young bilingual children can be viewed in terms of the choices the nursery staff make about how they relate to the children, how they structure each session, what children learn, what resources they provide and so on. However, these choices are partly pre-determined by educational tradition, passed on, for example, through training, by social and cultural values such as the aim of helping children learn to be independent, and by social policy which, for example, provides nursery places for all four year olds in England. So decisions taken by early years staff are no more than interpretations of an existing and finite context which has social approval.

The lack of training and guidance for early years staff working with young children learning English as an additional language has at least been recognised. Newly qualified teachers (NQTs) have voiced criticism over the lack of appropriate training in this field.

Developing knowledge and understanding about children learning EAL was highlighted by the TTA in the 2002 Standards (Teacher Training Agency, 2002) as a key area for students on ITE courses. It is also integral to promoting equality of opportunity in the early years. However, the draft revised TDA (Teacher Development Agency) standards for QTS from September 2007 diminish the issue of EAL by including it with special educational needs and disabilities, rather than as a distinctive area.

Implications for policy makers

Nonetheless, more attention is being paid to English as an additional language and its implications for equality of opportunity in the early years. The pace and extent of developments and changes in UK policy over the last decade have affected early years practice and provision a good deal. The context is now set for a continuing review of equality and diversity which takes into account the multi-disciplinary nature of services, the revised early years curriculum and a new emphasis on partnerships with parents. In the past, provision for bilingual children was regarded as a marginal issue. But there appears to be a change of focus and children learning English as an additional language have now become more central to policy initiatives.

Central to this focus are principles embodied in statutory requirements – for example, the Race Relations Amendment Act (2000) which established a statutory obligation for all institutions in the public sector, including schools, to have race equality policies which are acted on and monitored through Ofsted school inspections. Initiatives such as *SureStart* have improved matters, with emphasis on partnership with parents. So has the requirement that statutory providers in health and local education authorities work to- gether with local communities to identify need and provide intensive support for young children and their families.

A DfES consultation document, *Aiming High: Raising the Achievement of Minority Ethnic Pupils* (2003) declares the Government's intention to make minority ethnic achievement less marginal and more central to mainstream education and it identifies the need for training programmes to increase the competence and confidence of nursery teachers, teaching assistants and childcare workers.

Inclusion and equality are also central to the *Curriculum Guidance for the Foundation Stage* (2000). One of its key principles for early years education is that 'no child should be excluded or disadvantaged because of ethnicity, cul- ture or religion, home language, family background, special educational needs, disability, gender or ability'. The Guidance also recognises the diversity of children in early years settings and for the first time includes discrete sections on 'meeting the diverse needs of children' and 'children with English as an additional language'.

So matters may be improving in relation to policy since the time in 1984 when the author of the article quoted in Chapter 1 said: 'There is very little training for them [school support staff] and they are left to intuit the ethos of the school. This process is too haphazard for Rehana and all other children like her'.

Exploring the experiences of Nazma, Samia and Maria has revealed how little training there is still to help educational providers understand young bilin- gual children's learning. Yet the stories of these children and their families have important implications for early years practitioners and these need to be attended to for the sake of all the young bilingual children in our schools.

Nazma, Samia and Maria adjusted to the inadequate provision by adopting strategies which enabled them to set about learning the language and culture of early schooling and become agents of their own actions. Their need to suc- ceed in the education system and overcome underachievement is highlighted in Nazma's elder sister, Naseem's experience of schooling (see Chapter 1).

This concluding chapter summarises the three key frameworks outlined in Chapter 4. The stories contribute to a refined and extended theoretical framework in which to situate the nursery experience of children as they become bilingual in school. This is outlined and the role of cultural and linguistic mediators in bilingual children's early learning is considered. Finally, some of the implications of this research are set out for educators of young bilingual children and policy makers.

First, we look again at the task facing developing bilingual children from the socio-cultural perspective which informed my study, and point to the inter-relatedness of language, culture and socialisation. This study incorporated and extended the socio-cultural interpretation of agency by emphasising the key role of the child in the context of early schooling. The new dimension to this theoretical perspective is the way the young bilingual children take control of their learning of English in the contexts of home and school.

The role of the child in her own learning

The strategies used by Nazma, Maria and Samia emphasise, firstly, the child as agent, in control of her own learning. The language each needs to improve her chances of doing well at nursery and fulfil adult expectations could only be acquired through the language adults used with them and the other children. The language generated through interaction with children is crucial for their social well-being and for their learning through free and structured play activities. But this in itself is not enough to guarantee success in schooling.

Nazma, Samia and Maria had to engage with the learning expected by adults. This process required them to respond to adult questions, using materials in the appropriate way, participating in adult led activities and following the kinds of exploratory and repetitive practices prioritised in the curriculum for concept development. But it took time for each child to respond to adults with confidence, since the situation left them so exposed.

On the other hand, the girls practised their English with other children, as we saw, and rehearsed their new language when on their own. This is one of their key strategies for finding their way through nursery during the early years.

The control Nazma, Samia and Maria took over their learning was apparent in the strategies they adopted as they went through the process of learning English while experiencing formal schooling for the first time. But the detailed picture which emerged at home and in nursery was not visible to the nursery teacher and appeared therefore not be understood.

Nursery provision was similar for all three children. All attended multi-ethnic schools which had experienced teachers who planned and delivered a curriculum defined by current English education policy. Availability of BCA support to support bilingual children's transition from mother tongue to English, was similar in all three settings – about 8 hours per week.

Little that the system provided for any of the girls was in any way special. The same learning experiences were presented to bilingual children as were presented to all children. They were taught by adults in much the same way as the other children. The adults, as we saw, acted mostly with patience in response to the child's silent period, allowing time for her to orientate and catch up with her English speaking peers. But they were not in a position to offer more than that.

Although provision for all the children was broadly the same and the nursery environment was viewed as a good context for learning English, this study has yielded evidence to show that current early years policy and practice is not designed to meet the distinctive needs of bilingual children and is inadequate for the task. It demonstrates that the children need to design their own strategies in order to make their way through early schooling experiences and that some fare better than others.

Certain underlying factors enabled them to assert their own agency and develop their own strategies. The girls' mothers all expected their children to retain and develop their home language and culture. The aspiration of all three was that their children would excel in the English education system. For Nazma, her mother tongue was virtually the lifeline to learning. Without Pahari she would have been wholly isolated in the nursery. And Pahari gave Samia and Maria the linguistic platform from which they could launch into English for their early school learning: both used Pahari to effect their transition from home to school and both adapted rapidly to new linguistic circumstances as they arose. But it is highly possible that Maria and Samia will gain educational success at the expense of losing Pahari and that Nazma's strong attachment to Pahari portends poor attainment in school. As practitioners, we need to be aware of the tension these young children might encounter between two possibly irreconcilable pressures: to succeed within the system, and to satisfy the cultural and linguistic expectations of the home.

Maria and Samia understood the importance of engaging with all aspects of learning in the nursery. This is evident when the girls begin to engage in social interaction with peers. But these interactions took place in contexts and in safe places which were not observable by the teacher. Both Maria and Samia were willing to take risks and experiment with their English whilst playing with other children. Samia used the strategy of practising English in the bathroom with her friend, Bahriye. Maria pursued the strategy of rehearsing English during her play in a quiet corner of the nursery. As their confidence develops, we see Samia and Maria asking questions and using language play as strategies for engaging in play with other children at nursery.

The children's interactions with adults in the nursery are central in determining their relative success in the education system. Maria and Samia appear to understand the need to engage with the learning presented by adults and to achieve the results that adults expect, both at nursery and at home. Recognising the significance of responding appropriately to adults, Samia demonstrates her control by minimising risk-taking in her response to adults' expectations.

A particularly significant strategy for both Maria and Samia was to display their knowledge of colours, which they did in appropriate interactions with adults. And Samia demonstrated growing control over her learning by using her home language with a bilingual adult in the nursery, as well as at home with her mother and grandmother.

We saw how confident Maria was in her interactions with adults in both environments. During her early experiences of schooling she could act out a strategic role as centre of attention and take charge. She was even prepared to respond by taking risks. One of her key strategies was to use simple repetition to engage with adults. Taking on these roles allowed her to be viewed as a successful learner by the nursery staff. Recordings at home displayed her invisible use of mature English and mother tongue. She took a leading role in her learning at home and at school. On the other hand, Nazma enjoyed little social interaction with her teacher and her experience appears similar to the way her older sister struggled in the schooling system.

Being viewed as successful or unsuccessful at this stage has long term implications. Of most concern is the fact that the children's early interactions in the nursery appear to have a serious and lasting effect on their life chances. How well does current provision support children like Nazma, as they struggle to learn English in their early years of schooling? Our educational system urgently needs to focus policy and provision so that the disadvantages experienced by children like Nazma and Naseem are identified and addressed.

The cultural mediator has an especially significant role. We saw how the BCA could use the lifeline of Nazma's mother tongue to bring her home experiences into school learning and help her to make sense of nursery. It is the involvement of key agents such as Mussarat that will help us mediate, understand and contribute to constructing a new and meaningful curriculum for bilingual children.

The role of the bilingual adult

The interaction between Nazma and Mussarat (see Chapter 5) shows clearly the unique position of the BCA to mediate the new language and culture for Nazma. Nazma's language and knowledge of speech events in Pahari is adequate for her community and family needs. Indeed, at home she enjoys the full, normal linguistic environment essential for children's development of language. For her, it comes in the form of a language not well recognised by the educational system. When Nazma enters nursery she appears not to have the skills she needs to engage with the learning experiences. Yet for Samia and Maria these linguistic circumstances provide a good basis for a curriculum delivered exclusively in English. We saw that Nazma and her siblings are active participants in a range of activities at home, but these resources, or 'funds of knowledge' (Moll *et al*, 1992) of the child's world outside the classroom are rarely drawn on in school.

Thus bilingual staff have an important role in helping mediate a continuity between the cultural and linguistic expectations of home and school. Mussarat is able to bridge the gap between experiences in the home and those in the nursery. She uses her mother tongue for learning purposes in the nursery, and for talking to Nazma about her home experiences and communicating with her parents.

The official literature produced in England clearly fails to recognise the distinctive nature of teaching and learning English as an additional language adequately. And it is even less informative about the role of bilingual staff like Mussarat. For example, while there are Standards for teaching assistants which include reference to working with children learning EAL, there are to date no equivalent Standards for bilingual classroom assistants. As Bourne (2001: 253) observes: 'In general, bilingual assistants have had to make their own niche within the broad continuum of expectations for general classroom ancillary workers'. Also lacking is any guidance – or even research – on the use by BCAs of both mother tongue and English to support children's learning. Martin-Jones (1995) and Bourne (2001) are almost unique in drawing attention to the distinct and significant role of bilingual classroom assistants.

Bourne (2001) points to the professional isolation of bilingual classroom assistants and to the power asymmetry between the roles constructed for the class teacher and the BCA:

> Primary classrooms are social worlds of their own, creating special sorts of identities and ways of behaving for those who enter them. Each social space has its own patterns of legitimate behaviour and ways of speaking which constrain the participants' choices of social action'. (200: 256)

This comment applies to bilingual children and to bilingual classroom assistants alike. Despite the inclusion of the word 'bilingual' in the role title, not all BCAs feel comfortable about using children's home languages in the classroom. Bourne warns that '...the presence of an assistant who happened to be bilingual was no guarantee of bilingual language use' (2001: 255). But she stresses that the presence of a bilingual classroom assistant in a classroom has a significant impact:

> It is not always recognised that inserting bilingual support into what has up to now been a monolingual curriculum often entails that different cultures, different ideologies and practices of teaching are also brought into the classroom, along with the different languages. Bilingualism questions ethnocentrism. (2001: 262)

Bourne argues that in these circumstances not only will class teachers need to reconsider their practice but also that there is a wider need to:

> ... design a pedagogy in which bilingual support can have a place. But introducing bilingual support should entail a critical re-examination of the bases of recipes for primary practice. The prevailing power asymmetry between monolingual teachers and bilingual support assistants does not easily allow for exploration of different pedagogies and of the possibilities of emerging new forms of pedagogy. (Bourne, 2001: 263)

Transcripts of Mussarat's work with Nazma demonstrate that the support she gives is vital to Nazma's engagement in the nursery and doubtless to other Pahari speaking children. However, what Mussarat and others like her have achieved has been carried out without the intervention 'in the reconstruction of concepts of 'good practice" (2001: 266) which Bourne calls for.

The child mediating her own learning

The role of scaffolding, guided participation and synergy

Studies relating to scaffolding, guided participation and synergy focus on the adult as mediator (scaffolding and guided participation) or the synergy between older children using the language of school (see Chapter 4). This book provides insights into how young children play a key role in extending these concepts beyond the unequal relationship indicated in Rogoff's guided participation. It thus contributes new understandings of the notion of reciprocity interpreted in Gregory's theory of synergy by showing how, in the cases of three bilingual learners, children employ their own strategies for learning.

My study has revealed how this synergy and scaffolding begin amongst bilingual children at an early age, even though they have little command of the new school language. It draws on data which shows the interaction with a younger child in Samia's play at home with her younger brother (Chapter 2). The synergy or unique reciprocity whereby an older child 'teaches' her younger sibling and at the same time develops her own learning is clearly shown.

The same event reveals how much Samia was absorbing the everyday language used by adults in the nursery. This differs from the language she learned through social interaction with her peers. It also shows the extent to which she had absorbed the routines and expectations in the nursery setting. This cultural learning became vital to her, building her confidence in knowing what to do and how to behave, and was closely interwoven with her language learning. Her use of the language she heard from adults in the nursery in her play illustrates how her language learning and her developing socio-cultural positioning was related to taking on the 'voice' of influential others in a process of 'ventriloquation' (Bakhtin, 1986).

The role of asserting possession in the silent period

Studies of second language acquisition, as we saw in Chapter 4, view the silent period as principally passive. In studies by Wong Filmore (1979), Tabors (1997) and Clarke (1996) the silent period, the use of silent rehearsal of language and formulaic language have been recognised as normal processes. This information is helpful for practitioners' understanding. But self-assertion had not been recognised as playing a crucial role during this period – until now. It is right that self-assertion should be recognised as a normal response at the stage before early social language develops. Since such assertion could be interpreted negatively, early years staff need to know that self-assertion should be seen as a recognised and acceptable phase in the behaviour of children at an early stage of learning English.

The use of the strategy of self-assertion is a normal and important stage that children go through as they adjust to the new environment of early schooling and is a way of projecting their own identities before they develop further early social language.

The research informing this book specifically provides a new perspective on the silent period in the early development of English as an additional language. Previous studies into second language acquisition have established recognisable early stages in the learning of English and indeed acknowledge the silent period, but they do not expand its important implications for the wider socio-cultural context of young children's learning at home and at school.

The key aspects of learning for Nazma, Samia and Maria relate to mother tongue development, English language learning, social interaction, nursery routines and the learning encouraged through the nursery curriculum. The process of learning English is interwoven with these other aspects of learning. The children need social interaction in order to learn English – but at the same time they need English so they can engage with their peers. During their first term in nursery, the three children spend long periods listening actively to the English spoken by other children at play. However, the need to assert their identities and to use the strategy of asserting possession commands all their English language resources in the early transcripts. Using self-assertion, for example: 'no, mine; not yours', is a key strategy for getting by during their first few months in nursery.

Implications for practice

What will most help children like Nazma, Samia and Maria when they come to nursery, and how can practitioners support the highly motivated and active learning shown in this book? We conclude by indicating the practice that will be most beneficial for young early stage learners of English as they adjust to their new socio-cultural setting and most effective for ensuring their progress, while recognising the challenges.

Develop home school understandings

Practitioners need to draw on the bilingual children's home experiences and interests through:

- home visits, parents' involvement in the early years setting and discussion with bilingual adults
- planning for activities and interactions which are culturally and linguistically familiar.

Make the rules and routines explicit

Practitioners need to make the rules and routines of the setting explicit, consistent and predictable by:

- taking account of the values and cultural norms of children's home backgrounds
- making the aims and expectations of the early years provision explicit to the bilingual children and their parents
- seeking the parents' views and expectations for the education of their children

Support mother tongue development

Bilingual staff need to build on the bilingual children's cognitive development in the home context and their use of mother tongue in the following ways:

- Bilingual staff, or other bilingual adults, spend time on a planned basis using mother tongue for routine classroom interactions and to support learning
- the use of mother tongue in the early years setting is explicitly encouraged
- all adults in the nursery give a clear message about when and why mother tongue is being used
- include mother tongue support in the curriculum statement and the subject of the ongoing planning of provision.

Provide opportunities for one-to-one interaction with adults

Practitioners should provide frequent opportunities for interaction by:

- using sensitive questioning techniques to enable the child to engage with learning experiences
- adjusting to the child's language level, using repetition and taking time to assist with responses
- enabling known patterns to be practised and extending and expanding such patterns
- modelling language in the contextualised situation.

Provide opportunities for language learning in teacher-led small group work

Practitioners should provide opportunities for teacher-led group work through:

■ providing opportunities for joining in choral responses, responding in turn-taking discussions which repeat patterns of language, and listening to the interactions of other children with the teacher

■ ensuring that early stage learners are made to feel part of the group, even when the linguistic context is beyond their full understanding, and accepting their non-verbal responses

■ understanding the stage of English language development of bilingual learners in the group and being sensitive to contexts which enable them to respond or participate, and to contexts in which children can listen without having to respond

■ understanding the stage of self-assertion in the silent period when children are new to English and making allowance for children using this strategy.

Seek ways of supporting social interaction

Practitioners should provide opportunities to exploit language development by:

■ reducing the potential for stress in the new learning environment and maximising opportunities for participation

■ providing contexts which encourage English speaking children to interact with their bilingual peers to support English language learning and assist early stage learners to move beyond the double-bind and learn the social language they need for interaction

■ planning for the consistent inclusion of bilingual children in small group activities which enable interaction with peers in activities which promote communication.

There are pre-requisites to the practice suggested here.

■ The implementation of the practice suggested above demands a planned approach including physical layout of classrooms to facilitate private areas

■ The role of bilingual staff is critical and this means their full involvement in planning and policy development. There may be implications for training, recruitment and status. Their role needs to be seen as central rather than as peripheral to the learning of bilingual children in early years settings

■ A training programme will be required for all early years staff

■ The suggested points of effective practice which are specific to bilingual children need to be clearly presented in the revised QCA Early Years curriculum guidance and TDA Standards for teacher training.

Using multilingual methodologies in research

The ethnographic methodologies outlined in this book capture the children's bilingual voices at home and at school. They make clear how important it is to investigate practice from the perspective of the child, the family and community. The methodologies used here demonstrate ways of providing windows on young bilingual children's learning and shed light on how they participate in and contribute to multiple communities (see pages vii, viii and ix).

The interview with Nazma six years on, and presented early in the book offers valuable insights into her early experiences at nursery, and indicates the value of potential future longitudinal ethnographic studies of young children over years to give us a reflective perspective on early learning.

As a researcher I began as a reflective practitioner and developed my work through a network of fellow researchers involved in exploring the early learning experiences of young bilingual children. My research takes a socio-cultural perspective: children's learning is seen in the context of their home and community learning. This perspective allows me to view the social and cultural aspects of bilingual children's learning situation as integral to the record of their language and learning development. It takes account of the individual child's social and cultural heritage and their experience at home and recognises the importance of bilingualism in ultimately giving bilingual learners cognitive, social, linguistic and cultural advantages.

The statutory requirements and statements of principle made by policy makers have to be reflected in the policies of settings. However, it is only through the reflective expertise of practitioners and the adoption of multilingual methodologies such as those outlined in this book that policy can be appropriately structured and implemented for individual children with their diverse experiences and needs. Until this becomes common practice in schools, bilingual learners are at risk of losing out in education.

Glossary

BCA (Bilingual Classroom Assistant) The Swann Report (1985) recognised the value of providing unqualified ancillary staff as a 'bilingual resource' to 'help with the transitional needs of non-English speaking children starting school' (DES, 1985: 407). BCAs are staff paid hourly to support bilingual children at an early stage in their learning of English by using the child's home language to assist their learning. The presence of an adult who speaks the children's home language also helps children settle in school and enhances the school's communication with parents. BCAs normally work in the classroom under the direction of the class teacher

EAL English as an additional language (EAL) is preferred to English as a second language (ESL) because many bilingual pupils know more than one language in addition to their developing use of English. EAL has become the accepted term in the UK.

Bilingual pupils This term is usually used to describe pupils who understand and use two or more languages – home or community languages and also English. Bilingual pupils may have varying degrees of fluency in the languages they know. In this book the term includes children at an early stage in their learning of English.

Pahari Pahari is a dialect of Punjabi spoken by people in Azad Kashmir which borders North East Pakistan. Literally, it means 'hill language' in a region which has a number of dialects. Mirpuri is a dialect spoken in the district of Mirpur. Other districts, including Kotli, have their own Pahari dialects.

Pre-school Community-Based Project A pre-school project set up in Hertfordshire Minority Ethnic Community Support Service to help minority ethnic parents and their children in the community and school context. It aimed to increase the opportunities for young children to succeed in the school system. Bilingual outreach assistants were employed to visit homes and work with parents and children in their home language.

Bibliography

Anon (1984) Rehana's Reception. *Issues*, Autumn, 1984

Aubrey, C., David, T., Godfrey, R. and Thompson, L. (2000) *Early Childhood Educational Research: Issues in methodology and ethics*. London: Routledge/Falmer Press

Bakhtin, M.M. (1981) *The dialogic imagination: four essays by M. M. Bakhtin*. (M. Holquist, ed.; C. Emerson and M. Holquist, trans.). Austin: University of Texas Press

Bakhtin, M.M. (1986) *Speech genres and other late essays*. (C. Emerson and M. Holquist, eds., V.W. McGee, trans.). Austin: University of Texas Press

Bourne, J. (2001) Doing what comes naturally: how the discourses and routines of teachers' practice constrain opportunities for bilingual support in UK primary schools. *Language and Education*, Vol. 15, 4, 250-268

Bruner, J.S. (1983) *Child's Talk: learning to use language*. Oxford: Oxford University Press

Bruner, J.S. (1990) *Acts of Meaning*. Cambridge, MA: Harvard University Press

Clark, A. and Moss, P. (2001) *Listening to Young Children. The Mosaic Approach*. London: National Children's Bureau

Clark A., Kjorholt. A. T. and Moss, P. (eds.) (2005) *Beyond listening. Children's perspectives on early childhood services*. Bristol: The Policy Press

Clarke, P. (1992) *English as a 2nd Language in Early Childhood*. FKA Multicultural Resource Centre. Richmond: Victoria, Australia

Clarke, P. (1996) Investigating Second Language Acquisition in Preschools. Unpublished doctoral thesis. La Trobe University, Victoria, Australia

Cole, M. (1985) The zone of proximal development where culture and cognition create each other. In J.V. Wertsch (ed.) *Culture, communication and cognition: Vygotskian perspectives*. Cambridge: Cambridge University Press

Connolly, P. (1998) *Racism, Gender Identities and Young Children: Social relations in a multi-ethnic Inner city primary school*. London: Routledge

Crystal, D. (1987) *Child Language, Learning and Linguistics*. London: Arnold

Department for Education and Skills (2003) *Aiming High: Raising the Achievement of Minority Ethnic Pupils*. London: DfES

Department of Education and Science (1975) *A Language for Life* (The Bullock Report) London: HMSO

Drury, R. (1997) Two sisters at school: issues for educators of young bilingual children, in: Gregory, E. (1997) *One Child, Many Worlds: Early Learning in Multicultural Communities*. London: David Fulton

Fetterman, D. (1989) *Ethnography Step by Step*. Newbury Park, CA: Sage

Gregory, E. (1993) Sweet and Sour: Learning to read in British and Chinese school. *English in Education* 27(3)

Gregory, E. and Williams, A. (2000) *City Literacies: learning to read across generations and cultures*. London: Routledge

Gregory, E. (2001) Sisters and brothers as language and literacy teachers: Synergy between siblings playing and working together. *Journal of Early Childhood Literacy*, 1 (3) 301-322

Griffiths, M. (1998) *Educational Research for Social Justice: getting off the fence*. Buckingham: Open University Press

Hammersley, M. and Atkinson, P. (1983) *Ethnography: Principles in Practice*. London: Methuen

Haste, H. (1987) Growing into rules. In Bruner, J. and Haste, H. (eds.) *Making sense: The child's construction of the world*. London: Methuen

Hirschler, J. (1994) Preschool children's help to second language learners, *Journal of Educational Issues of Language Minority Students*, 14, 227-240

Holquist, M. and Emerson, C. (1981) *Glossary for the Dialogic Imagination: Four essays by M. M. Bakhtin*, ed. Holquist, M.. Trans. Holquist, M. and Emerson, C. Austin: University of Texas Press

Krashen, S. D. (1985) *The Input Hypothesis: Issues and implications*. London: Longman

MacNaughton, G., Rolfe, S.A., Siraj-Blatchford, I. (2001) *Doing Early Childhood Research: International perspectives on theory and practice*. Buckingham: Open University Press

Martin-Jones, M. (1995) Codeswitching in the classroom: two decades of research. In Milroy, L. and Muysken, P. (Eds.) *One Speaker, Two Languages*. Cambridge: Cambridge University Press

Moll, L.C., Amanti, C., Neff, D. and Gonzalez, N. (1992) Funds of knowledge for teaching: using a qualitative approach to connect homes and classrooms. *Theory Into Practice*, Vol. XXX1, No.2, Spring 1992

NALDIC (National Association for Language Development in the Curriculum) (1998) *Guidelines on Baseline Assessment for Bilingual Children*. Working Paper 4. Watford: NALDIC

Pollard, A. with Filer, A. (1996) *The Social World of Children's Learning: Case studies of pupils from four to seven*. London: Cassell

Pollard, A. (2000) Child Agency and Primary Schooling. In Boushel, M., Fawcett, M. and Selwyn, J. (eds.) *Focus on Early Childhood Principles and Realities*. Oxford: Blackwell Science.

QCA (Qualifications and Curriculum Authority) (2000) *Curriculum Guidance for the Foundation Stage*. London: Qualifications and Curriculum Authority

Rogoff, B. (1990) *Apprenticeship in Thinking: cognitive development in social context*. New York: Oxford University Press

Rogoff, B., Mosier, C., Mistry, J. and Goncu, A. (1998) Toddlers' guided participation with their caregivers in cultural activity. In M. Woodhead, D. Faulkner and K. Littleton (eds.) *Cultural Worlds of Early Childhood*. London: Routledge

Saville-Troike, M. (1988) Private speech: Evidence for second language learning strategies during the 'silent period', *Journal of Child Language*. 15, 567-590

Spindler, G. (1982) *Doing the Ethnography of Schooling: Educational anthropology in action*. New York: CBS College Publishing

Spradley, J.P. and McCurdy, D.W. (1990) *Conformity and Conflict: Readings in cultural anthropology*. New York: Harper Collins

Street, C. and Street, B.(1993) The schooling of literacy. In Murphy, P., Selinger, M., Bourne, J., and Briggs, M. (eds) *Subject Learning in the Primary Curriculum: Issues in English, science and mathematics*. London and New York in association with the OU: Routledge

Swann, M. (1985) *Education for All*. London: HMSO

Tabors, P. (1997) *One Child, Two Languages: a guide for preschool educators of children learning English as a second language*. Baltimore: Paul Brookes Publishing

Teacher Training Agency (2002) *Qualifying to Teach Handbook of Guidance Autumn 2002*. London:TTA

Thompson, L. (1999) *Young Bilingual Learners in Nursery School*. Clevedon: Multilingual Matters

Vygotsky, L.S. (1978) *Mind in Society: the development of higher psychological processes*. M. Cole, V. John-Steiner, S. Scribner, and E. Souberman, eds.Cambridge, MA: Harvard University Press

Wertsch, J.V. (1991) *Voices of the mind: a sociocultural approach to mediated action*. Hemel Hempstead: Harvester Wheatsheaf

Wertsch, J.V., Tulviste, P. and Hagstrom F. (1993) A sociocultural approach to agency. In Forman, E., Mimick, N. and Addison Stone, C. *Contexts for Learning Sociocultural Dynamics in Children's Development*. Oxford: Oxford University Press

Willett, J. (1995) Becoming first graders in an L2 classroom: An ethnographic study of L2 socialisation. *TESOL Quarterly*, 29, 473-503

Wood, D., Bruner, J.S. and Ross, G. (1976) The role of tutoring in problem solving. *Journal of Child Psychology and Psychiatry*, 17, 89-100

Wood, D. (1998) Aspects of teaching and learning. In M. Woodhead, D. Faulkner and K. Littleton (eds.) *Cultural Worlds of Early Childhood*. London: Routledge

Wong Fillmore, L. (1979) Individual differences in second language acquisition. In Fillmore, C.J., Kempler, D. and Wang W. S-Y. (1979) (Eds) *Individual Differences in Language Ability and Language Behaviour*. New York: Academic Press

Index